THE POETRY OF CATULLUS

J.S.

THE POETRY OF

CATULLUS

Translated by C. H. Sisson

With the complete Latin text

The Orion Press · New York · 1967

PUBLISHED BY GROSSMAN PUBLISHERS, INC.
PUBLISHED IN ENGLAND BY MACGIBBON & KEE LTD. 1966

MANUFACTURED IN THE UNITED STATES OF AMERICA
LIBRARY OF CONGRESS CATALOGUE CARD NO. 66-26543

ACKNOWLEDGMENT

Edgar Betterton, who is a better scholar than I and has long been a student of Catullus, read the typescript and made a number of valuable suggestions, all of which threw light on the text and most of which I used. Where I did not use them it was simply because a translator, in the end, has to insist on his own pig-headedness.

I have generally followed the Loeb text, and in all cases the numbering of that edition. This accounts for the jump from XVII to XXI.

INTRODUCTION

CATULLUS QUOQUE ELEGANTISSIMUS POETARUM (Aulus Gellius, Noct. Attic. VII, 20). He was born at Verona, 84 B.C. or about then, and he died when he was thirty, i.e., about 54 B.C. The country north of the Po was then a province, Cisalpine Gaul; it was not until a few years after Catullus's death that the inhabitants acquired the full rights of Roman citizenship. Verona had been a Gallic town, but must be supposed to have been more or less completely Romanized by the time Catullus knew it.

Catullus's family was well off. They entertained the governor of the province, which was no doubt expensive. It was natural that when Catullus went to Rome, where he settled, he should mix in the best society and consequently feel poor. His life is described in his poems or, if it is not, we know nothing about it. He made at least one long journey out of Italy, to Bithynia, where he joined the staff of Memmius who was propraetor. There are verses to bear witness that he was profoundly touched by the visit to his brother's tomb in the Troad, and by the association with the spot where Europe and Asia met. Of course for him this was the site of the Trojan War. By habit very much a metropolitan Roman, the remoter frontiers of the world were often in his imagination (VII, XLVI, LXIII, LXV, LXVIIIA, CI).

It was the world of Julius Caesar. Caesar, who was perhaps sixteen years his senior, was that governor of Cisalpine Gaul whom his father entertained; Catullus was near enough to the man who was remaking the world to see the man as well as his public actions. By some commentators Catullus is supposed to have had an unaffected admiration for Cicero; I do not read XLIX that way. It would have been surprising if he had been at the feet of that man of so many words, who as well as being an orator was a versifier in a tradition Catullus was in the process of extinguishing.

I am not competent to discuss the nature of the literary revolution Catullus effected. It has been the subject of studies by a contemporary scholar (K. F. Quinn, *The Catullan Revolution*). Catullus was a student of the Alexandrian poets; there are numerous references to Callimachus (Battiades), and LXVI is a translation of a poem of Callimachus of which some fragments remain. The attractions of Alexandrian sophistication, at the point in Roman literary history when Ennius and Plautus were being relegated, are obvious enough. Most significant for us, 'Catullus has evolved a style that appears not just simple and direct, but frequently slangy and at times ostentatiously obscene.' (R. F. Quinn, in *Critical Essays on Roman Literature*, edited by J. P. Sullivan, 1962, p. 47.)

The obscenity of Catullus has long been a stumbling block. There are now perhaps those for whom any obscenity is, *prima facie*, the mark of a good thing. They are far from understanding the mind of Catullus. On the other hand it will not do to talk of 'poems which do not lend themselves to comment in English' and omit them, as C. J. Fordyce does—admittedly in an edition (1961) intended for universities and schools. The poems have produced some comic blushes in grown-up scholars. Nettleship (*Lectures and Essays*, 1885, p. 93) says:

> 'But, as Mr. Munro wisely warns us, the kind of charges brought by Catullus against Caesar are in no way to be taken seriously.'

—'in no way' is rather rich—

> 'It cannot be too often repeated that much of the indecency of the classical poets and orators was purely conventional, and carried no slur on the character either of the writer who uttered it or of the person whom he attacked.'

Alexander Guarinus (1521) was probably better placed to understand his author. I have not had access to a copy of his commentary, but it was extensively used by Robinson Ellis, of whose work (1876) it is impossible to speak too highly, and who says of him:

> 'No doubt modern taste is offended by the plainness, not to say grossness of his explanations; which indeed perpetually suggest that he was illustrating the corruptions of Catullus' time by observations drawn from his own.

Reading Catullus one is brought face to face with the Roman world. By Vergil and Horace the blinds were drawn; they tried to make out that the human race was all right, as the *divus Augustus* made out that he had achieved an eternal political settlement. In the world of Julius Caesar the lid was off; and Catullus is, among other things, the poet of that age. His charges (*pace* Nettleship) are to be taken seriously. The legionaries sang:

> Ecce Caesar nunc triumphat, qui subegit Gallias.
> Nicomedes non triumphat, qui subegit Caesarem.

The sexual morals of the ancient world are not those of our own. Two things alone—and there are others—serve to make an absolute difference: the existence of slavery and the fact that Christianity had, if I may so express myself, not yet been invented. The birth of Christ was an event, not to be denied by us who come afterwards, however we squirm.

The poems of Catullus are full of personal allusions. There is no need to insist on those which relate to Lesbia, whether she was Clodia or another like her. There is even more radical concern with Eros, and one is left wondering what the gods meant to a sophisticated Roman, as they were fading. Obviously LXIII (*The Attis*) is a crucial poem. It has the air of having a high personal import; what that was we cannot exactly know. The worship of the Magna Mater had been introduced into Rome during the Second Punic War (218–202 B.C.), and Catullus's friend Caecilius wrote a poem on the same subject (XXXV). One may still have the suspicion that the life of Catullus's poem owes something to the breath of the east he must have felt in Bithynia, and something to a more personal experience, there or elsewhere.

PREFACE

Catullus walked in the Campus Martius.
He had seen all he needed to see,
Lain on his bed at noon, and got up to his whore.
His heart had been driven out of his side
By a young bitch—well, she was beautiful,
Even, while the illusion was with him, tender.
She had resolved herself into splayed legs
And lubricity in the most popular places.
He had seen Caesar who—had he not been, once,
The drunken pathic of the King of Bithynia?—
Returning in triumph from the western isles:
Nothing was too good for this unique emperor.
Against these fortunes he had nothing to offer
—Possibly the remains of his indignation,
A few verses that would outlive the century.
His mind was a clear lake in which he had swum:
There was nothing but to await a new cloud.
We have seen it. But Catullus did not;
He had already hovered his thirty years
On the edge of the Mediterranean basin.
The other, rising like a whirlwind in a remote province,
Was of a character he would have ignored.
And yet the body burnt out by lechery,
Turning to its tomb, was awaiting this,
Fore-running as surely as John the Baptist
An impossible love pincered from a human form.

THE POETRY OF CATULLUS

I

Cui dono lepidum novum libellum
arida modo pumice expolitum?
Corneli, tibi: namque tu solebas
meas esse aliquid putare nugas,
iam tum cum ausus es unus Italorum
omne aevum tribus explicare chartis
doctis, Iuppiter, et laboriosis.
quare habe tibi quicquid hoc libelli,
qualecumque; quod, o patrona virgo,
plus uno maneat perenne saeclo.

II

Passer, deliciae meae puellae,
quicum ludere, quem in sinu tenere,
cui primum digitum dare appetenti
et acris solet incitare morsus
cum desiderio meo nitenti
carum nescio quid lubet iocari,
credo ut, cum gravis acquiescet ardor,
sit solaciolum sui doloris,
tecum ludere sicut ipsa possem
et tristis animi levare curas!

IIA

Tam gratumst mihi quam ferunt puellae
pernici aureolum fuisse malum,
quod zonam soluit diu ligatam.

I

To whom shall I offer this charming new volume,
Just smartened up with dry pumice?
Cornelius, to you: for you have been accustomed
To think that there is something in my trifles
Since the time when you, alone of the Italians,
Were bold to explain all ages in three volumes;
They were learned books, produced with much industry.
So take and keep for yourself this little book,
Whatever it amounts to. And Patroness, Virgin,
May it still be read after more than one century.

II

Sparrow my Lesbia likes to play with,
The one she likes to hold in her lap
To whom she gives her finger tip
To make him bite, as she likes, more sharply,
When, shining because of my desire
She finds it a precious thing to play with
(I think, when her grave fire acquiesces
She finds it a solace for her pain).
If I could play with you just as she does
I'd have a way of lightening my cares.

IIA

This is as sweet as the golden apple
Was, so they say, to Atalanta:
It loosed her girdle too long tied up.

III

Lugete, o Veneres Cupidinesque,
et quantumst hominum venustiorum.
passer mortuus est meae puellae,
passer, deliciae meae puellae,
quem plus illa oculis suis amabat:
nam mellitus erat suamque norat
ipsam tam bene quam puella matrem:
nec sese a gremio illius movebat,
sed circumsiliens modo huc modo illuc
ad solam dominam usque pipiabat
qui nunc it per iter tenebricosum
illuc, unde negant redire quemquam.
at vobis male sit, malae tenebrae
Orci, quae omnia bella devoratis:
tam bellum mihi passerem abstulistis.
o factum male! o miselle passer!
tua nunc opera meae puellae
flendo turgiduli rubent ocelli.

IV

Phasellus ille quem videtis, hospites,
ait fuisse navium celerrimus,
neque ullius natantis impetum trabis
nequisse praeter ire, sive palmulis
opus foret volare sive linteo.
et hoc negat minacis Hadriatici
negare litus insulasve Cycladas
Rhodumque nobilem horridamque Thraciam
Propontida, trucemve Ponticum sinum,
ubi iste post phasellus antea fuit

III

Time for mourning, Loves and Cupids
And any man of wit and love.
The sparrow's dead, my girl's own sparrow
That she loved more than her eyes:
For it was sweeter and knew her better
Than any girl might know her mother;
The bird would not move from her lap!
But hopping here and hopping there
Chirped for its mistress, no one else.
Now it goes to the darkened pathway
Out of which, they say, none comes back.
But curses on you, cursed darkness,
Orcus, you eat everything up.
You have taken my little sparrow away.
Oh, badly done! Oh, poor little bird!
It's all your doing, my poor girl's eyes
Are heavy and red with weeping now.

IV

That yacht, as I was telling my guests,
Regards herself as the fastest of ships.
There is nothing afloat that she could not pass
Whether she was driven with oars or sail.
She says that the windy Adriatic will agree,
The Cyclades, Rhodes and the bleak Thracian strait,
Or the dark bay of Pontus
Where, before she was a boat, she was long-haired woodland:

comata silva: nam Cytorio in iugo
loquente saepe sibilum edidit coma.
Amastri Pontica et Cytore buxifer,
tibi haec fuisse et esse cognitissima
ait phasellus; ultima ex origine
tuo stetisse dicit in cacumine,
tuo imbuisse palmulas in aequore,
et inde tot per impotentia freta
erum tulisse, laeva sive dextera
vocaret aura, sive utumque Iuppiter
simul secundus incidisset in pedem;
neque ulla vota litoralibus deis
sibi esse facta, cum veniret a mari
novissimo hunc ad usque limpidum lacum.
sed haec prius fuere: nunc recondita
senet quiete seque dedicat tibi,
gemelle Castor et gemelle Castoris.

V

Vivamus, mea Lesbia, atque amemus,
rumoresque senum severiorum
omnes unius aestimemus assis.
soles occidere et redire possunt:
nobis cum semel occidit brevis lux,
nox est perpetua una dormienda
da mi basia mille, deinde centum,
dein mille altera, dein secunda centum,
deinde usque altera mille, dinde centum
dein, cum milia multa fecerimus,
conturbabimus illa, ne sciamus,
aut nequis malus invidere possit,
cum tantum sciat esse basiorum.

For on Cytorus, on the hill-back,
She gave out a rustling with her speaking leaves.
Pontic Amastris and Cytorus
Green with box, all these, she says, were well known to her.
From her beginning she stood on that summit;
It was here she first dipped oars;
And from there she brought me over so many uncontrolled seas
To port or starboard as the wind called
Or with Jove blowing astern on both sheets;
And she had never cried mercy from any god ashore
When she came from the last salt to this limpid lake.
But these events are past: now, hidden away,
She grows old quietly, offering herself up
To the twin Castor and to Castor's brother.

V

Living, dear Lesbia, is useless without loving:
The observations of the censorious old
Are worth a penny every piece of advice.
One day follows another, the sun comes back
But when once we have gone away we do not;
Once night comes for us, it is night for ever.
Give me a thousand kisses, and then a hundred,
Then give me a second thousand, a second hundred
And then another thousand, and then a hundred
And when we have made up many, many thousands
Let us forget to count. Better not to know—
It will bring someone's jealous eye upon us
If people know we give so many kisses.

VI

Flavi, delicias tuas Catullo,
ni sint illepidae atque inelegantes,
velles dicere, nec tacere posses.
verum nescio quid febriculosi
scorti diligis: hoc pudet fateri.
nam te non viduas iacere noctes
nequiquam tacitum, cubile clamat
sertis ac Syrio fragans olivo,
pulvinusque peraeque et hic et illic
attritus, tremulique quassa lecti
argutatio inambulatioque.
nam nil stupra valet, nihil, tacere.
cur? non tam latera ecfututa pandas,
ni tu quid facias ineptiarum
quare quicquid habes boni malique.
dis nobis. volo te ac tuos amores
ad caelum lepido vocare versu.

VII

Queris, quot mihi basiationes
tuae, Lesbia, sint satis superque.
quam magnus numerus Libyssae harenae
lasarpiciferis iacet Cyrenis,
oraclum Iovis inter aestuosi
et Batti veteris sacrum sepulcrum,
aut quam sidera multa, cum tacet nox,
furtivos hominum vident amores,
tam te basia multa basiare
vesano satis et super Catullost,
quae nec pernumerare curiosi
possint nec mala fascinare lingua.

VI

Flavius, I know that you would tell me your pleasures
If they were not—shall we say?—a bit on the rough side;
If they were not, you would not know how to keep quiet.
It is obvious to me that you have chosen some female
Not quite in condition, and that no doubt makes you silent.
But you don't lie alone; that is plain as such a thing need be.
Your bed cannot speak, but it shouts: it has garlands,
Is scented with Syrian olives, the bolsters and pillows
Pressed down, thrown this way and that; it is shaken,
It is tremulous, goes up and down. So nothing, but nothing
Can possibly hide what you're up to. When you flop down exhausted
It is plain that you do so because of your amorous diversions.
So tell us whatever you've done. And was it successful?
I should very much like to make Flavius and Flavius's pleasures
The subject of some of my more agreeable verses.

VII

You ask me, Lesbia, how many kisses
Make enough kisses for me to take from you.
As many as there are sands in the desert
In Libya, the drugged sands of Cyrenaica
Between the oracle of that burning Jove
And the monument of the mythical Battus;
As many as there are stars, in the quiet night
Looking on furtive copulations.
That would be kisses enough for Catullus
To kiss you with, that would be more than enough:
A number which could neither be counted by the inquisitive
Nor put under any spell by malevolent tongues.

VIII

Miser Catulle, desinas ineptire,
et quod vides perisse perditum ducas.
fulsere quondam candidi tibi soles,
cum ventitabas quo puella ducebat
amata nobis quantum amabitur nulla.
ibi illa multa tum iocosa fiebant,
quae tu volebas nec puella nolebat.
fulsere vere candidi tibi soles.
nunc iam illa non vult: tu quoque.
impotens, noli,
nec quae fugit sectare, nec miser vive,
sed obstinata mente perfer, obdura.
vale, puella. iam Catullus obdurat,
nec te requiret nec rogabit invitam:
at tu dolebis, cum rogaberis nulla.
scelesta, vae te. quae tibi manet vita?
quis nunc te adibit? cui videberis bella?
quem nunc amabis? cuius esse diceris?
quem basiabis? cui labella mordebis?
at tu, Catulle, destinatus obdura.

IX

Verani, omnibus e meis amicis
antistans mihi milibus trecentis,
venistine domum ad tuos Penates
fratresque unanimos anumque matrem?
venisti. o mihi nuntii beati!
visam te incolumem audiamque Hiberum

VIII

You had better stop playing the fool, Catullus,
And accept that what you see is lost, is lost.
Once your days were shining
When you used to go wherever the girl led you,
She loved as none will ever be loved.
Then those many pleasant things were done
Which you wanted and the girl was willing to do;
Certainly then your days were shining.
She wants those things no more: you had better not want them,
Nor ask for what will not be given, nor live in pain.
Be patient, harden your mind.
Good-bye, girl. Already Catullus is hardened.
He does not seek you, and will not, since you are unwilling.
But you will suffer when you are asked for nothing at night.
It is the end. What life remains for you?
Who now will come to you? Who will think you pretty?
Whom will you now love? Whose will you say you are?
Whom will you kiss? And whose lips will you bite?
But you, Catullus, accept fate and be firm.

IX

Veranius, of all my friends
The best of all of them
And are you here again?
Back to your aged mother and
Your unanimous brothers?
Those messengers were welcome!
And shall I see you safe,
Talking over Iberia

narrantem loca, facta, nationes,
ut mos est tuus, applicansque collum
iucundum os oculosque saviabor.
o quantumst hominum beatiorum,
quid me laetius est beatiusve?

X

Varus me meus ad suos amores
visum duxerat e foro otiosum,
scortillum, ut mihi tum repente visumst,
non sane illepidum neque invenustum.
huc ut venimus, incidere nobis
sermones varii; in quibus, quid esset
iam Bithynia, quo modo se haberet,
ecquonam mihi profuisset aere.
respondi id quod erat, nihil neque ipsis
nec praetoribus esse nec cohorti
cur quisquam caput unctius referret,
praesertim quibus esset irrumator
praetor, nec faceret pili cohortem.
"at certe tamen," inquiunt, "quod illic
natum dicitur esse, comparasti
ad lecticam homines." ego, ut puellae
unum me facerem beatiorem,
"non" inquam "mihi tam fuit maligne,
ut, provincia quod mala incidisset,
non possem octo homines parare rectos."
at mi nullus erat nec hic neque illic,
fractum qui veteris pedem grabati
in collo sibi collocare posset.
hic illa, ut decuit cinaediorem,
"quaeso" inquit "mihi, mi Catulle, paulum

Its places, facts and peoples
As your way is; draw your neck to me
And kiss your smiling mouth and eyes?
No one is luckier than I
At this moment, or happier.

X

Varus had taken me from the Forum
Where I was idling, to see his mistress,
Not at all a bad little whore, as it seemed to me
—Quite good looking.
When we got there we started talking
About various things; among them what sort of place
Bythinia was now, how things were going there,
In particular, whether I had made any money.
I said how it was, that there was nothing in it
Either for ourselves, the praetor or his cohort,
To enable anyone to come back with his hair well oiled—
Especially since the praetor was a bastard,
Not caring a damn for his cohort.
Still, they said, you must have got a few men to carry your litter
That's the country they come from.
I, to make myself out to be one of the lucky ones,
Answered that I hadn't managed things so badly
Poor as the province was
That I couldn't find eight men who could stand upright.
In fact I had no one, in Rome or in Bythinia,
Who could lift the broken leg of a camp bed on his back.
The girl said—what can you expect of a whore?—
Would you be kind enough to lend me those men

istos: commodum enim volo ad Sarapim
deferri." "mane" inquii puellae;
"istud quod modo dixeram me habere.
fugit me ratio: meus sodalis
—Cinnast Gaius—is sibi paravit.
verum, utrum illius an mei, quid ad me?
utor tam bene quam mihi paratis.
sed tu insulsa male ac molesta vivis,
per quam non licet esse neglegentem."

XI

Furi et Aureli, comites Catulli,
sive in extremos penetrabit Indos,
litus ut longe resonante Eoa
tunditur unda,

sive in Hyrcanos Arabasve molles,
seu Sagas sagittiferosque Parthos,
sive quae septemgeminus colorat
aequora Nilus,

sive trans altas gradietur Alpes,
Caesaris visens monimenta magni,
Gallicum Rhenum, horribilesque ulti-
mosque Britannos,

omnia haec, quaecumque feret voluntas
caelitum, temptare simul parati,
pauca nuntiate meae puellae
non bona dicta.

To take me just as far as the temple of Serapis?
Half a minute, I said to the girl,
When I said that just now I was forgetting
They actually belong to Gaius Cinna.
Of course, whether they are his or mine, it's all the same,
I use them as if they were my own.
But you are a nasty tactless creature, you are
One can't make the slightest mistake without getting into trouble.

XI

Furius and Aurelius, friends of Catullus,
Whether he has a mind to go to India
Where the eastern ocean beats upon the shore
Echoing far off

Or to the Hyrcanians and the soft Arabians,
To the Scythians or the arrow-bearing Parthians,
Or to those plains which the sevenfold Nile
Dyes with its mud.

Whether he will climb across the High Alps
To view the memorials of great Caesar,
The Gallic Rhine, or the ultimate recesses
Of the barbarous Britons.

Ready although you are to do all these things
And indeed anything else that the fates direct
The service I ask is only that you take a message,
Not a very nice one.

cum suis vivat valeatque moechis,
quos simul complexa tenet trecentos,
nullum amans vere, sed identidem omnium
ilia rumpens:

nec meum respectet, ut ante, amorem,
qui illius culpa cecidit velut prati
ultimi flos, praeter eunte postquam
tactus aratrost.

XII

Marrucine Asini, manu sinistra
non belle uteris in ioco atque vino:
tollis lintea neglegentiorum.
hoc salsum esse putas? fugit te, inepte:
quamvis sordida res et invenustast.
non credis mihi? crede Pollioni
fratri, qui tua furta vel talento
mutari velit: est enim leporum
disertus puer ac facetiarum.
quare aut hendecasyllabos trecentos
expecta aut mihi linteum remitte;
quod me non movet aestimatione,
verumst mnemosynum mei sodalis.
nam sudaria Saetaba ex Hiberis
miserunt mihi muneri Fabullus
et Veranius: haec amem necessest
ut Veraniolum meum et Fabullum.

Tell my girl to enjoy herself with her lechers,
I hope she may manage three hundred at one time,
Not loving any properly, but leaving all of them
With ruptured arteries.

Tell her not to expect my love any more
And that it is through her fault that it has fallen
Like a flower at the edge of a meadow
When the plough passes.

XII

Marrucinus Asinius, your left hand
Could be better employed at table
Than in stealing people's napkins.
Do you think that a joke? It is an extremely poor one,
About as silly and witless as such a thing can be.
If you don't believe me, perhaps you will believe Pollio,
Your brother, who would give a talent to buy you off from your thieving,
For he has a better idea of what is amusing.
So now you will get three hundred hendecasyllables
Unless you send me back my napkin;
It is not for the value of the thing in money
But because it reminds me of my friends.
Fabullus and Veranius sent me some Saetaban napkins
As a present from Iberia
And I am as fond of them, necessarily
As I am of Veranius and Fabullus.

XIII

Cenabis bene, mi Fabulle, apud me
paucis, si tibi di favent, diebus,
si tecum attuleris bonam atque magnam
cenam, non sine candida puella
et vino et sale et omnibus cachinnis.
haec si, inquam, attuleris, venuste noster,
cenabis bene: nam tui Catulli
plenus sacculus est aranearum.
sed contra accipies meros amores
seu quid suavius elegantiusvest:
nam unguentum dabo, quod meae puellae
donarunt Veneres Cupidinesque,
quod tu cum olfacies, deos rogabis,
totum ut te faciant, Fabulle, nasum.

XIV

Ni te plus oculis meis amarem,
iucundissime Calve, munere isto
odissem te odio Vatiniano:
nam quid feci ego quidve sum locutus,
cur me tot male perderes poetis?
isti di mala multa dent clienti,
qui tantum tibi misit impiorum.
quod si, ut suspicor, hoc novum ac repertum
munus dat tibi Sulla litterator,
non est mi male, sed bene ac beate,
quod non dispereunt tui labores.
di magni, horribilem et sacrum libellum,
quem tu scilicet ad tuum Catullum
misti, continuo ut die periret

If your ill mind and rapacious fury
Carry you on to such a point
That you do not stop at this injury
Then you shall suffer, with feet tied up
And mullet and radishes stuck up your arse.

XVI[1]

All right I'll bugger you and suck your pricks
Aurelius and Furius, you pair of sodomites
Who imagine, on the strength of my verses
That I am lacking in reserve as they are.
But although the sacred poet ought to be chaste
It does not follow that his verses should be.

XVII

So the Colony would like a long bridge,
One they can dance on, but fear the rickety
Joints of the one they have got, patched with second hand timber,
Which might collapse and sink in the depths of the marsh.
You can have as good a bridge as you wish,
One fit even for the rites of Salisubsilus,
If you will give me the chance of a good laugh.
There is one of my fellow citizens I should like to see
Go head-over-heels from your bridge into the mud,
In the deepest, most stinking place of the whole marsh.

[1] See note, page 187.

insulsissimus est homo, nec sapit pueri instar
bimuli tremula patris dormientis in ulna.
cui cum sit viridissimo nupta flore puella—
et puella tenellulo delicatior haedo,
asservanda nigerrimis diligentius uvis,—
ludere hanc sinit ut lubet, nec pili facit uni,
nec se sublevat ex sua parte, sed velut alnus
in fossa Liguri iacet suppernata securi,
tantundem omnia sentiens quam si nulla sit usquam,
talis iste meus stupor nil videt, nihil audit,
ipse qui sit, utrum sit an non sit, id quoque nescit.
nunc eum volo de tuo ponte mittere pronum,
si pote stolidum repente excitare veternum
et supinum animum in gravi derelinquere caeno,
ferream ut soleam tenaci in voragine mula.

XXI

Aureli, pater esuritionum,
non harum modo, sed quot aut fuerunt
aut sunt aut aliis erunt in annis.
pedicare cupis meos amores.
nec clam: nam simul es, iocaris una,
haerens ad latus omnia experiris.
frustra: nam insidias mihi instruentem
tangam te prior irrumatione.
atque id si faceres satur, tacerem:
nunc ipsum id doleo, quod esurire
me me puer et sitire discet.
quare desine, dum licet pudico,
ne finem facias, sed irrumatus.

He is a man with no more sense than a small boy,
A two-year-old rocked to sleep by his father.
He has married a girl in the very flower of her youth;
The girl is more delicate than a tender kid,
She deserves to be kept like a bunch of the blackest grapes
And he lets her play as she will, and is quite indifferent.
He does not stir himself, but lies like a log
In the ditch where it has been felled by a Ligurian axe.
With as much sensation as if nothing existed, anywhere,
The clot sees nothing, he hears nothing;
What he is, whether he is or not, he does not know.
Now he is the man I should like to throw from your bridge
To see whether he can be roused from his lethargy.
And leave his supine mind in the dirty sludge,
Much as a mule might leave her shoe in the mire.

XXI

Aurelius, father of hungers,
Not of these only, but of all that were
Or are, or will be in other years,
You want to turn pederast with my boy.
Not surreptitiously; you are with him, you joke together,
You stick beside him and leave nothing untried.
It is no good you plotting against me,
I'll see you buggered first.
If you were satisfied I would say nothing;
As it is, you teach my boy to have an appetite.
Leave off while you may do so with decorum
Lest you end up buggered.

XXII

Suffenus iste, Vare, quem probe nosti,
homost venustus et dicax et urbanus,
idemque longe plurimos facit versus.
puto esse ego illi milia aut decem aut plura
perscripta, nec sic ut fit in palimpsestos
relata: chartae regiae, novi libri,
novi umbilici, lora rubra, membranae,
derecta plumbo, et pumice omnia aequata.
haec cum legas tu, bellus ille et urbanus
Suffenus unus caprimulgus aut fossor
rursus videtur: tantum abhorret ac mutat.
hoc quid putemus esse? qui modo scurra
aut siquid hac re tritius videbatur,
idem infacetost infacetior rure,
simul poemata attigit; neque idem umquam
aequest beatus ac poema cum scribit:
tam gaudet in se tamque se ipse miratur.
nimirum idem omnes fallimur, nequest quisquam
quem non in aliqua re videre Suffenum
possis. suus cuique attributus est error:
sed non videmus manticae quod in tergost.

XXIII

Furi, cui neque servus est neque arca
nec cimex neque araneus neque ignis,
verumst et pater et noverca, quorum
dentes vel silicem comesse possunt,
est pulcre tibi cum tuo parente
et cum coniuge lignea parentis.
nec mirum: bene nam valetis omnes,

XXII

Suffenus, Varus, whom you know so well,
Is not only witty, polite, acceptable,
He even writes more verses than other people.
I believe he has at least ten thousand, perhaps more,
All copied out, not just on bits of paper
—Royal parchment, beautiful bindings,
Lines ruled with lead, and all smoothed out with pumice.
But when you read him, the elegant Suffenus
Turns out to be a goatherd or a ditcher,
He is so unlike himself, so changed.
What can one make of it? This charming wit,
This expert in civilized conversation
Is about as dull as a row of turnips
One he touches poetry. However
He is never so happy as when he is writing it;
Then he can love himself and admire his talents.
Still, we all imagine that we have gifts,
And everyone is a bit like Suffenus;
Everyone has his special delusion—
Our view of ourselves is a bit different from other people's.

XXIII

Furius, you have no slave, no money,
Not a bug, not a spider, and no fire;
You have, however, a father and a stepmother
Whose teeth could eat up flint-stones.
It is delightful, the life you lead with those two,
The old man and his mahogany wife.
No wonder; you all enjoy good health;

pulcre concoquitis, nihil timetis,
non incendia, non graves ruinas,
non furta impia, non dolos veneni,
non casus alios periculorum.
atiqui corpora sicciora cornu
aut siquid magis aridumst habetis
sole et frigore et esuritione.
quare non tibi sit bene ac beate?
a te sudor, abest, abest saliva,
mucusque et mala pituita nasi.
hanc ad munditiem adde mundiorem,
quod culus tibi purior salillost,
nec toto decies cacas in anno,
atque id durius est faba et lapillus;
quod tu si manibus teras fricesque,
non unquam digitum inquinare possis.
haec tu commoda tam beata, Furi,
noli spernere nec putare parvi,
et sestertia quae soles precari
centum desine; nam sat es beatus.

XXIV

O qui flosculus es Iuventiorum,
non horum modo, sed quot aut fuerunt
aut posthac aliis erunt in annis,
mallem divitias Midae dedisses
isti, cui neque servus est neque arca,
quam sic te sineres ab illo amari.
"quid? non est homo bellus?" inquies. est:
sed bello huic neque servus est neque arca.
hoc tu quamlubet abice elevaque:
nec servum tamen ille habet neque arcam.

Your digestions are good; you fear nothing,
Not fire, or houses falling on your head.
Or thieving, or plots to poison you
Or other occasions of danger.
But your bodies, drier than bones
Or anything drier you can think of,
Are made so by sun, cold and hunger.
Why should you not be well and contented?
You have no sweat, no saliva;
Your noses are absolutely free from snot.
To this purity one may add a more impressive one:
Your anus is cleaner than a saltcellar.
You don't shit ten times in a whole year
And then it is harder than beans or pebbles.
If you press it or rub it with your hands
You can't even dirty your fingers.
You should not scorn advantages like that, Furius,
Or reckon them to be small ones.
You should stop asking for a hundred sestertia,
Really you are well off enough already.

XXIV

O flower of the Juventii, not only
Of those now living, but your ancestors
And those who will be in the years to come,
I would rather you gave the riches of Midas
To that man without slave or money
Than that you should allow him to love you.
'Well, is he not polite?' you ask. He is:
But this polite man has neither slave nor money.
You can say it does not matter if you will;
The fact remains, he has neither slave nor money.

XXV

Cinaede Thalle, mollior cuniculi capillo
vel anseris medullula vel imula oricilla
vel pene languido senis situque araneoso,
idemque Thalle, turbida rapacior procella,
remitte pallium mihi meum, quod involasti,
sudariumque Saetabum catagraphosque Thynos,
inepte, quae palam soles habere tamquam avita
quae nunc tuis ab unguibus reglutina et remitte,
ne laneum latusculum manusque mollicellas
inusta turpiter tibi flagella conscribillent,
et insolenter aestues velut minuta magno
deprensa navis in mari vesaniente vento.

XXVI

Furi, villula nostra non ad Austri
flatus oppositast neque ad Favoni
nec saevi Boreae aut Apheliotae,
verum ad milia quindecim et ducentos.
o ventum horribilem atque pestilentem!

XXVII

Minister vetuli puer Falerni
inger mi calices amariores,
ut lex Postumiae iubet magistrae,
ebrioso acino ebriosioris.
at vos quolubet hinc abite, lymphae,
vini pernicies, et ad severos
migrate: hic merus est Thyonianus.

XXV

Thallus you pansy, softer than rabbit's wool,
The down of a goose or the lobe of an ear,
Softer than an old man's penis and the cobwebs hanging from it.
Thallus none the less rapacious as the wind,
Give me back my cloak, you stole it,
And my Saetaban napkins and Bythynian tablets.
You clot, you show them off as if they were heirlooms.
Unstick your claws from them and send them back
Or you may find your dear little body and hands
Inscribed in shameful fashion by a horsewhip
And yourself tossing around in an unusual way
Like a small ship caught in an enormous storm.

XXVI

My little villa is exposed to the blast
Not of the south wind or the west wind
Or even of the north wind or the east wind
But of fifteen thousand two hundred sestertia,
A horrible and pestilential wind.

XXVII

You are looking after the Falernian
So pour me out stronger cups;
I am sure Postumia would tell you to do so;
She is fuller of wine than a grape herself.
The water can go as far away as it likes;
It ruins wine, it had better trickle off to the sober.
This is pure Thyonian.

XXVIII

Pisonis comites, cohors inanis
aptis sarcinulis et expeditis,
Verani optime tuque mi Fabulle,
quid rerum geritis? satisne cum isto
vappa frigoraque et famem tulistis?
ecquidnam in tabulis patet lucelli
expensum, ut mihi, qui meum secutus
praetorem refero datum lucello
"o Memmi, bene me ac diu supinum
tota ista trabe lentus irrumasti."
sed, quantum video, pari fuistis
casu: nam nihilo minore verpa
farti estis. pete nobiles amicos!
at vobis mala multa di deaeque
dent, opprobria Romuli Remique.

XXIX

Quis hoc potest videre, quis potest pati,
nisi impudicus et vorax et aleo,
Mamurram habere quod Comata Gallia
habebat ante et ultima Britannia?
cinaede Romule, haec videbis et feres?
[es impudicus et vorax et aleo.]
et ille nunc superbus et superfluens
perambulabit omnium cubilia
ut albulus columbus aut Adoneus?
cinaede Romule, haec videbis et feres?
es impudicus et vorax et aleo.
eone nomine, imperator unice,
fuisti in ultima occidentis insula,

XXVIII

You who have been with Piso, which is not the way to grow rich,
Have no difficulty with your baggage, it is easily lifted;
Veranius and Fabullus, I am glad to see you, how are you?
Were you cold and hungry enough with that sour bastard?
Were all your winnings in the wrong direction
As mine were, when I was with my praetor?
My only credits were debits.
Memmius, you had me down and properly buggered,
Slowly, with your whole great beam.
You two seem to have been in like case,
Filled up with a prick of the same size.
Friends in high places!
May the gods and goddesses give you every kind of bad luck,
Blots on the names of Romulus and Remus.

XXIX

Who can see this, who can suffer this,
Except the shameless, the rapacious, the gambler—
Mamurra in possession of what before
The hairy Gaul had and the far-off Briton?
Depraved Romulus, can you see this and bear it?
Now he walks proud in his superfluity
Through everyone's beds like a leching pigeon
Or a handsome Adonis.
Depraved Romulus, can you see it and bear it?
It is because you are shameless, voracious, a gambler.
Was it for this, unique emperor,
That you went to the last island of the west?

ut ista vostra diffutata Mentula
ducentiens comesset aut trecentiens?
quid est alid sinistra liberalitas?
parum expatravit an parum helluatus est?
paterna prima lancinata sunt bona:
secunda praeda Pontica: inde tertia
Hibera, quam scit amnis aurifer Tagus.
hunc Galliae timet et Britanniae
quid hunc malum fovetis? aut quid hic potest.
nisi uncta devorare patrimonia?
eone nomine urbis opulentissime
socer generque, perdidistis omnia?

XXX

Alfene immemor atque unanimis false sodalibus
iam te nil miseret, dure, tui dulcis amiculi?
iam me prodere, iam non dubitas fallere, perfide?
num facta impia fallacum hominum caelicolis placent?
quae tu neglegis, ac me miserum deseris in malis;
eheu quid faciant, dic, homines, cuive habeant fidem?
certe tute iubebas animam tradere, inque, ⟨me⟩
inducens in amorem, quasi tuta omnia mi forent.
idem nunc retrahis te ac tua dicta omnia factaque
ventos irrita ferre ac nebulas aerias sinis.
si tu oblitus es, at di meminerunt, meminit Fides,
quae te ut paeniteat postmodo facti faciet tui.

Was it so that this worn-out codpiece Mamurra
Could squander twenty or thirty million?
What is that but the liberality of a pervert?
Has he spent little on lust and gluttony?
First he ran through his paternal estate,
The spoils of Pontus next, then those of Spain.
You should hear what is said in the Tagus gold fields.
Is this the man feared throughout Gaul and Britain?
Why do you keep such a man?
He is a general devourer of patrimonies.
Is it for this you and Pompey have thrown away everything?

XXX

You forget your friends, Alfenus, you let them down,
You have no pity for me, though we have been close.
Betrayal, deception, seem to you quite normal?
You think this sort of thing pleases the gods?
It seems so, and you desert me in my need.
What can men do, in whom are they to trust?
You told me I could rely on you, it is unfair
Leading me on to love, as if all were safe.
Now you draw back and all your words and deeds
Are carried into nothing like the clouds and winds.
You may forget, the gods will not forget;
Faith will remember and you will suffer for it.

XXXI

Paene insularum, Sirmio, insularumque
ocelle, quascumque in liquentibus stagnis
marique vasto fert uterque Neptunus,
quam te libenter quamque laetus inviso,
vix mi ipse credens Thyniam atque Bithynos
liquisse campos et videre te in tuto.
o quid solutis est beatius curis,
cum mens onus reponit, ac peregrino
labore fessi venimus larem ad nostrum
desideratoque acquiescimus lecto?
hoc est, quod unumst pro laboribus tantis.
salve, o venusta Sirmio, atque ero gaude:
gaudete vosque, o Lydiae lacus undae:
ridete, quicquid est domi cachinnorum.

XXXII

Amabo, mea dulcis Ipsithilla.
meae deliciae, mei lepores,
iube ad te veniam meridiatum.
et si iusseris, illud adiuvato,
nequis liminis obseret tabellam,
neu tibi lubeat foras abire.
sed domi maneas paresque nobis
novem continuas fututiones.
verum, siquid ages, statim iubeto:
nam pransus iaceo, et satur supinus
pertundo tunicamque palliumque.

XXXI

Of all peninsulas and islands
The inner and the outer Neptune
Bear upon lakes or the great sea
Sirmio is delectable. With what pleasure
I see it again, hardly believing that I have left
The plains of Thynia and Bythinia.
What is more pleasant than to dispense with trouble?
The mind puts down her load and, tired with travel,
We come to our Lares and rest in our own beds.
This is really all we undertake these toils for.
Elegant Sirmio, I salute you.
Be glad your master has come.
Be glad, waters of the Lydian lake.
Laugh, whatever laughter there is in the house.

XXXII

Please darling, dear Ipsithilla,
All my pleasure, my only attraction,
Order me to you this afternoon
And if you do order me, please arrange also
That no one shall get in my way as I enter
And don't you go off either at the last moment.
But stay at home and organize for us
Nine copulations in rapid series.
If there's anything doing, send round immediately
For here I am, lying on my bed;
I have had my lunch, the thing sticks out of my tunic.

XXXIII

O furum optime balneariorum
Vibenni pater et cinaede fili,
nam dextra pater inquinatiore,
culo filius est voraciore:
cur non exilium malasque in oras
itis, quandoquidem patris rapinae
notae sunt populo, et nates pilosas,
fili, non potes asse venditare.

XXXIV

Dianae sumus in fide
puellae et pueri integri:
Dianam pueri integri
  puellaeque canamus.

o Latonia, maximi
magna progenies Iovis,
quam mater prope Deliam
  deposivit olivam,

montium domina ut fores
silvarumque virentium
saltuumque reconditorum
  amniumque sonantum.

tu Lucina dolentibus
Iuno dicta puerperis,
tu potens Trivia et notho's
  dicta lumine Luna.

XXXIII

The most accomplished thieves at the baths
Are old Vibennius and his pansy son;
The father has the dirtier hands,
The son the more voracious anus.
Why not go into exile now?
Since everyone knows about father's thieving
And, honestly, son, you'll never sell
Your hairy buttocks for more than tuppence.

XXXIV

We are Diana's children,
Girls not yet adolescent,
Boys not yet adolescent;
We sing Diana, Diana.

O Latonian, O noble
Daughter of Jove, your mother
Dropped you beneath the Delian
Olive, beneath the olive

So that you might be mistress
Of mountains and bursting woodland,
The mistress of hidden valleys
And echoing, echoing rivers.

You are called Juno Lucina
By women moaning in childbed;
You are called Trivia, and powerful
And Moon with the counterfeit light.

tu cursu, dea, menstruo
metiens iter annuum
rustica agricolae bonis
    tecta frugibus exples.

sis quocumque tibi placet
sancta nomine, Romulique,
antique ut solita's, bona
    sospites ope gentem.

XXXV

Poetae tenero, meo sodali
velim Caecilio, papyre, dicas
Veronam veniat, Novi relinquens
Comi moenia Lariumque litus:
nam quasdam volo cogitationes
amici accipiat sui meique.
quare, si sapiet, viam vorabit,
quamvis candida miliens puella
euntem revocet manusque collo
ambas iniciens roget morari;
quae nunc, si mihi vera nuntiantur,
illum deperit impotente amore:
nam quo tempore legit incohatam
Dindymi dominam, ex eo misellae
ignes interiorem edunt medullam.
ignosco tibi, Sapphica puella
Musa doctior: est enim venuste
Magna Caecilio incohata Mater.

Goddess, you measure the annual
Course of the year with your cycles;
You fill up the farm and the cottage
With your beneficent produce.

With whatever name you may favour
Be hallowed, and may you continue,
As you did in the past, so in future,
Your comfort and help to the Romans.

XXXV

I ask this paper to tell Caecilius,
The tender poet, and my friend,
To come to Verona and leave New Como
And leave the shores of Larius.
For there are certain cogitations
I want to put to him from a friend.
If he is wise he will certainly come
However often his candid girl
Calls him back and, throwing her two arms
Round his neck, implores him to stay.
She now, if all that I hear is true,
Loves him with lunatic desperation
For since the time she read the beginning
Of his poem on Cybele, the fire has been eating
Away at the poor girl's inmost marrow.
But I forgive you, you wiser Sappho,
It's perfectly true they're extremely good,
The opening lines of the 'Magna Mater.'

XXXVI

Annales Volusi, cacata charta,
votum solvite pro mea puella:
nam sanctae Veneri Cupidinique
vovit, si sibi restitutus essem
deissemque truces vibrare iambos,
electissima pessimi poetae
scripta tardipedi deo daturam
infelicibus ustulanda lignis.
et haec pessima se puella vidit
iocosis lepide vovere divis.
nunc, o caeruleo creata ponto,
quae sanctum Idalium Uriosque apertos
quaeque Ancona Gnidumque harundinosam
colis quaeque Amathunta quaeque Golgos
quaeque Durachium Hadriae tabernam,
acceptum face redditumque votum,
si non illepidum neque invenustumst.
at vos interea venite in ignem,
pleni ruris et infacetiarum
annales Volusi, cacata charta.

XXXVII

Salax taberna vosque contubernales,
a pilleatis nona fratribus pila,
solis putatis esse mentulas vobis,
solis licere, quidquid est puellarum,
confutuere et putare ceteros hircos?
an, continenter quod sedetis insulsi
centum an ducenti, non putatis ausurum
me una ducentos irrumare sessores?

XXXVI

Annals of Volusius, fresh from the lavatory,
Discharge the promise my girl made.
She made a vow to Venus and Cupid
That if I were given back to her
And ceased to brandish my sharp iambics
She, for her part, would give to Vulcan
The choicest works of the worst of poets
To be burnt with wood from an unlucky tree.
Now, goddess born of the blue, blue ocean,
You who inhabit sacred Idalium,
The bubs of Uria, Ancona,
Reedy Cnidos, Amathus, Golgos,
Dyrrhachium, the Adriatic drink-shop,
Chalk this vow up as one completed
Unless it seem to you in poor taste;
But meanwhile, you lot, into the fire
—Full of crudity, full of witlessness—
Annals of Volusius, from the lavatory.

XXXVII

Less pub than brothel, and you, the regulars
The ninth pillar from Castor and Pollux
Do you think you are the only ones equipped with a penis,
That you are the only ones licensed for fucking
And that the rest who do it are merely goats?
Do you think, as you sit waiting in rows
A hundred or two hundred together, that I shall not dare
To do the whole lot of you, two hundred together?

atqui putate: namque totius vobis
frontem tabernae scorpionibus scribam.
puella nam mi, quae meo sinu fugit,
amata tantum quantum amabitur nulla,
pro qua mihi sunt magna bella pugnata,
consedit istic. hanc boni beatique
omnes amatis, et quidem, quod indignumst
omnes pusilli et semitarii moechi;
tu praeter omnes une de capillatis.
cuniculosae Celtiberiae fili
Egnati, opaca quem bonum facit barba
et dens Hibera defricatus urina.

XXXVIII

Malest, Cornifici, tuo Catullo,
malest, me hercule, et laboriose,
et magis magis in dies et horas.
quem tu, quod minimum facillimumquest,
qua solatus es allocutione?
irascor tibi. sic meos amores?
paulum quid lubet allocutionis,
maestius lacrimis Simonideis.

Think again: I will draw scorpions
All over the walls of the place.
For my girl, who has escaped from my arms,
Who was loved as much, and more than any is loved,
For whom I have expended all my forces,
She is there. You, the great and the good, all love her,
You the valueless, corrupt, adulterous all love her;
You above all Egnatius
Long-haired son of a rabbit-toothed Celtiberian,
Only made good by your beard
Your teeth whitened by Spanish piss.

XXXVIII

Things go badly with me, Cornificius;
They go badly all right, they are more excruciating
Every day and every hour.
Easy for you to console me if you will, but you will not.
A few words, that is all that is needed.
I am angry with you. Is that how you treat my love?
Why will you not utter a few words of comfort,
A small poem, with a few tears, like Simonides?

XXXIX

Egnatius, quod candidos habet dentes,
renidet usquequaque. si ad rei ventumst
subsellium, cum orator excitat fletum,
renidet ille. si ad pii rogum fili
lugetur, orba cum flet unicum mater,
renidet ille. quicquid est, ubicumquest,
quodcumque agit, renidet. hunc habet morbum,
neque elegantem, ut arbitror, neque urbanum.
quare monendum test mihi, bone Egnati.
si urbanus esses aut Sabinus aut Tiburs
aut porcus Umber aut obesus Etruscus
aut Lanuvinus ater atque dentatus
aut Transpadanus, ut meos quoque attingam,
aut quilubet, qui puriter lavit dentes,
tamen renidere usquequaque te nollem:
nam risu inepto res ineptior nullast.
nunc Celtiber es: Celtiberia in terra,
quod quisque minxit, hoc sibi solet mane
dentem atque russam defricare gingivam;
ut quo iste vester expolitior dens est,
hoc te amplius bibisse praedicet loti.

XL

Quaenam te mala mens, miselle Ravide,
agit praecipitem in meos iambos?
quis deus tibi non bene advocatus
vecordem parat excitare rixam?
an ut pervenias in ora vulgi?
quid vis? qualubet esse notus optas?
eris, quandoquidem meos amores
cum longa voluisti amare poena.

XXXIX

Egnatius, because he has white teeth,
Smiles all the time. In court,
When the lawyers are reducing everyone to tears,
He smiles. At a funeral,
When a mother is mourning the death of an only son,
He smiles. Whatever is happening, anywhere,
Whatever he is doing, he smiles. He has this disease,
Not an elegant one, I think, nor very polite,
Let me give you warning, Egnatius.
If you were a city man or a Sabine or Tiburtine,
A pig of an Umbrian or a fat Etruscan,
Or a dark Lanuvian with a fine set of teeth,
Or a Transpadane (not to forget my own people)
Or anyone else with reasonable oral hygiene,
Still I shouldn't really want you to smile all the time
For nothing is stupider than a stupid smirk.
But you are a Celtiberian. Now the Celtiberians
Are accustomed to rub their teeth and gums every morning
With their matutinal micturations
So that, the more highly polished your teeth are,
We must assume, the more piss you drink.

XL

What folly, you wretched Ravidus,
Throws you into the path of my iambics?
What god have you stupidly invoked
To work up to an idiotic quarrel?
Do you want to be talked about? What do you want?
A little notoriety, no matter how it is come by?
You shall have it. You have set your desire where mine is;
The penalty shall be enduring.

XLI

Ameana puella defututa
tota milia me decem poposcit,
ista turpiculo puella naso,
decoctoris amica Formiani.
propinqui, quibus est puella curae,
amicos medicosque convocate:
non est sana puella, nec rogare
qualis sit solet aes imaginosum.

XLII

Adeste, hendecasyllabi, quot estis
omnes undique, quotquot estis omnes.
iocum me putat esse moecha turpis,
et negat mihi vestra redditura
pugillaria, si pati potestis.
persequamur eam, et reflagitemus.
quae sit, quaeritis. illa, quam videtis
turpe incedere, mimice ac moleste
ridentem catuli ore Gallicani.
circumsistite eam, et reflagitate,
"moecha putida, redde codicillos,
redde, putida moecha, codicillos."
non assis facis? o lutum, lupanar,
aut si perditius potes quid esse.
sed non est tamen hoc satis putandum.
quod si non aliud potest, ruborem
ferreo canis exprimamus ore:
conclamate iterum altiore voce
"moecha putida, redde codicillos,
redde, putida moecha, codicillos."

XLI

Ameana, the worn-out bitch,
Is asking for a whole ten thousand,
That girl with the flattened nose
That used to go with the Formian bankrupt.
Her family, or whoever looks after the girl
Had better call in her friends and doctors:
The girl is mad, she has never enquired
What a mirror would have to say about her.

XLII

I can do with hendecasyllables,
All the lot of them, as many as they like.
The filthy whore has thought of a joke:
She will not give my tablets back,
Which is more than a little hard to bear.
Better follow her, better beg them back.
Who is she? Over there, there she is,
Strutting like an actress and grinning like a cur.
Now surround her, and now call for them:
'Give them back, dirty bitch,
Give back the tablets, dirty bitch.'
You don't care? You shit, you whorehouse,
Or any improvement on those terms.
But it's no good thinking that is enough.
Oh well, if we get nothing else
Let's force a blush from the bitch's muzzle.
Shout together, but louder this time:
'Give them back, dirty bitch,
Give back the tablets, dirty bitch.'

sed nil proficimus, nihil movetur.
mutandast ratio modusque vobis,
siquid proficere amplius potestis:
"pudica et proba, redde codicillos."

XLIII

Salve, nec minimo puella naso
nec bello pede nec nigris ocellis
nec longis digitis nec ore sicco
nec sane nimis elegante lingua,
decoctoris amica Formiani.
ten Provincia narrat esse bellam?
tecum Lesbia nostra comparatur?
o saeclum insapiens et infacetum!

XLIV

O funde noster, seu Sabine seu Tiburs,
(nam te esse Tiburtem autumant, quibus non est
cordi Catullum laedere: at quibus cordist,
quovis Sabinum pignore esse contendunt)
sed seu Sabine sive verius Tiburs,
fui libenter in tua suburbana
villa, malamque pectore expuli tussim,
non immerenti quam mihi meus venter,
dum sumptuosas appeto, dedit, cenas.
nam, Sestianus dum volo esse conviva,
orationem in Antium petitorem
plenam veneni et pestilentiae legi.
hic me gravedo frigida et frequens tussis

But nothing happens, there's not a movement,
The method of asking had better be changed.
If you want to make progress you'd better try:
'Chaste and honest, give them back!'

XLIII

Girl with the not inconsiderable nose,
Sizable feet and eyes not exactly jet-black.
With fingers scarcely long and mouth which can hardly be called dry,
And a tongue you are in the habit of sticking out,
You who go to bed with the Formian bankrupt:
You are reported in the Province to be beautiful?
My Lesbia is compared with you?
What an uncultivated age we live in!

XLIV

My farm, either Sabine or Tiburtine
(Those who do not want to annoy me call it Tiburtine,
Those who do, bet anything it is Sabine)
—But whether it is Sabine or Tiburtine
I was glad enough to be there, more or less in the country,
And to get rid of my horrible cold on the chest.
My belly had given it to me, not undeservedly,
While I was trying to get to a rather splendid dinner.
For, wanting to be invited to Sestius,
I read his speech *In Antium petitorem*
—It is full of poison and undoubtedly infectious.
Anyway I had a shocking head and coughed all the time

quassavit usque dum in tuum sinum fugi
et me recuravi otioque et urtica.
quare refectus maximas tibi grates
ago, meum quod non es ulta peccatum.
nec deprecor iam, si nefaria scripta
Sesti recepso, quin gravedinem et tussim
non mi, sed ipsi Sestio ferat frigus,
qui tunc vocat me, cum malum librum legi.

XLV

Acmen Septimius suos amores
tenens in gremio "mea" inquit "Acme,
ni te perdite amo atque amare porro
omnes sum assidue paratus annos
quantum qui pote plurimum perire,
solus in Libya Indiaque tosta
caesio veniam obvius leoni."
hoc ut dixit, Amor, sinistra, ut ante
dextra, sternuit approbationem.
at Acme leviter caput reflectens
et dulcis pueri ebrios ocellos
illo purpureo ore saviata
"sic" inquit "mea vita Septimille,
huic uni domino usque serviamus,
ut multo mihi maior acriorque
ignis mollibus ardet in medullis."
hoc ut dixit, Amor, sinistram ut ante,
dextram sternuit approbationem.
nunc ab auspicio bono profecti
mutuis animis amant amantur.
unam Septimius misellus Acmen
mavolt quam Syrias Britanniasque:

And this went on till I got back to my farm
And a course of idleness and stinging nettles.
Now I am better, I am thankful the farm apparently forgave me.
If ever I look at those beastly compositions of Sestius again
I hope the cold will produce a frightful head and a cough
Not in me, in Sestius himself
Who only asks me when I have read one of his stupid books.

XLV

Septimius, Septimius holding Acme
In his arms, says to her: 'Acme, Acme,
If I don't love you, hopeless and headlong
And go on loving you for ever and ever
As much as ever, in desperation,
I hope I may end in Libya or India,
Eaten alive by a green-eyed lion'.
At this Love gave, to left and right hand,
Two small sneezes of approbation.
Acme, however, turning her head round
And kissing the sweet boy's fluttering eyelids
With her red, red lips, said: 'Septi darling,
I swear, I swear, as we serve one Cupid
My fire is worse, for my bones are tingling.'
At this Love gave, this time left-handed,
A further small sneeze of approbation.
Starting from these most favorable omens
They live together and love one another,
Poor young Septimius fonder of Acme
Than of all the wealth of Britain or Syria;

uno in Septimio fidelis Acme
facit delicias libidinesque.
quis ullos homines beatiores
vidit, quis Venerem auspicatiorem?

XLVI

Iam ver egelidos refert tepores,
iam caeli furor aequinoctialis
iucundis Zephyri silescit auris.
linquantur Phrygii, Catulle, campi
Niceaeque ager uber aestuosae:
ad claras Asiae volemus urbes.
iam mens praetrepidans avet vagari,
iam laeti studio pedes vigescunt.
a dulces comitum valete coetus,
longe quos simul a domo profectos
diversae varie viae reportant.

XLVII

Porci et Socration, duae sinistrae
Pisonis, scabies famesque munda,
vos Veraniolo meo et Fabullo
verpus praeposuit Priapus ille?
vos convivia lauta sumptuose
de die facitis? mei sodales
quaerunt in trivio vocationes?

Acme finding in poor Septimius
All she could want of amorous pleasure.
Who ever saw such a pair for loving
Or imagined that Venus could be so docile?

XLVI

Already it is spring, the days are warmer;
The fury of the equinoctial sky
Gives way to gentle breezes, Zephyrus.
Catullus, now they leave the Phrygian plains,
Nicaea, with its rich and burning fields:
Now I can see the famous towns of Asia.
My mind is trembling at the thought of travel;
I am so eager that my feet feel strong.
I say good-bye to all the friendly cohort
Who came together from their far-off home
And wander back through individual ways.

XLVII

Procius and Socration, two left hands of Piso,
Who operate like scurvy and famine
Has ballocky Priapus preferred you
To my Veranius and Fabullus?
Are you eating and drinking with the rich
In the middle of the afternoon while my friends
Wander the streets and wait to be sent for?

XLVIII

Mellitos oculos tuos, Iuventi,
siquis me sinat usque basiare,
usque ad milia basiem trecenta,
nec mi umquam videar satur futurus,
non si densior aridis aristis
sit nostrae seges osculationis.

XLIX

Disertissime Romuli nepotum,
quot sunt quotque fuere, Marce Tulli,
quotque post aliis erunt in annis,
gratias tibi maximas Catullus
agit pessimus omnium poeta,
tanto pessimus omnium poeta
quanto tu optimus omnium's patronus

L

Hesterno, Licini, die otiosi
multum lusimus in meis tabellis,
ut convenerat esse delicatos.
scribens versiculos uterque nostrum
ludebat numero modo hoc modo illoc,
reddens mutua per iocum atque vinum.
atque illinc abii tuo lepore
incensus, Licini, facetiisque,
ut nec me miserum cibus iuvaret
nec somnus tegeret quiete ocellos,

XLVIII

If I should be allowed to go as far as kissing
Your sweet eyes, Juventius,
I would go on kissing them three hundred thousand times
Nor would it ever seem I had had enough,
Not if I harvested
Kisses as numerous as the ears of standing corn.

XLIX

You are the best orator, Marcus Tullius,
There is or ever was among the Romans,
The best orator they ever will have.
Catullus tenders you his warmest thanks,
Catullus, who is the worst of all the poets
—As much the worst of all poets
As you are the best of all orators.

L

Yesterday, Licinius, was an idle day:
We amused ourselves with my tablets,
Giving ourselves up to being agreeable.
In turn we wrote verses in different meters,
Simply as something to go with the laughter and wine
But I came away so alight with your wit,
Lucinius, and the pleasure of these diversions,
That I was not interested in food
And sleep could not cover my eyes with quiet

sed toto indomitus furore lecto
versarer, cupiens videre lucem,
ut tecum loquerer simulque ut essem.
at defessa labore membra postquam
semimortua lectulo iacebant,
hoc, iucunde, tibi poema feci,
ex quo perspiceres meum dolorem.
nunc audax cave sis, precesque nostras
oramus cave despuas, ocelle,
ne poenas Nemesis reposcat a te.
est vemens dea: laedere hanc caveto.

LI

Ille mi par esse deo videtur,
Ille, si fas est, superare divos,
qui sedens adversus identidem te
spectat et audit
dulce ridentem, misero quod omnis
eripit sensus mihi; nam simul te,
Lesbia, aspexi, nihil est super mi
lingua sed torpet, tenuis sub artus
flamma demanat, sonitu suopte
tintinant aures, gemina teguntur
lumina nocte.

But, uncontrollably, from one side of the bed to the other,
I tossed and turned, longing to see the light
So that I could be with you and talk.
But when I was worn out with this activity
And lay on the bed hardly conscious,
I made this poem for you, agreeable friend.
You can see from that the nature of my pain.
Take care: if I beg and pray do not spit,
There is always Nemesis, my darling,
Who may well get her own back on you.
She is a difficult goddess; beware of annoying her.

LI

He seems like a god, that man,
He seems to subdue the gods, if I may put it that way;
He is sitting opposite you and yet repeatedly
Looks at you and hears
Your delightful laughter. I should be completely senseless.
When I look at you, Lesbia, there is nothing left of my voice.
My tongue is frozen, a thin flame descends through my limbs,
There is ringing in my ears, my two eyes
Are covered with night.

LIa

Otium, Catulle, tibi molestumst:
otio exultas nimiumque gestis.
otium et reges prius et beatas
perdidit urbes.

LII

Quid est, Catulle? quid moraris emori?
sella in curuli Struma Nonius sedet,
per consulatum perierat Vatinius:
quid est, Catulle? quid moraris emori?

LIII

Risi nescio quem modo e corona,
qui, cum mirifice Vatiniana
meus crimina Calvus explicasset,
admirans ait haec manusque tollens,
"di magi, salaputtium disertum!"

LIV

Otonis caput (oppidost pusillum)
et Eri rustice semilauta crura,
subtile et leve peditum Libonis,
si non omnia, displicere vellem
tibi et Fuficio seni recocto.

LIa

Leisure is no good to you, Catullus;
You are elevated and perform extravagantly.
Leisure has destroyed kings before now
And cities that have been so fortunate.

LII

What reason is there for not dying, Catullus?
Nonius nurses his wen in the curule chair;
Vatinius perjures his way into the consulship.
What reason is there for not dying, Catullus?

LIII

I laughed at that chap in the crowd:
When Calvus was holding forth in his best manner
About the series of charges against Vatinius,
He listened admiringly and lifting up his hands
Said, 'Gods, what a clever little cock he is!'

LIV

Otho's head is a very little one,
It is as if Erius had waded in from a pigsty,
While Libo has a trick of lifting his leg.
It is impossible that you should like everything about them,
You and Fuficius, that old man warmed up.

LIVa

Irascere iterum meis iambis
immerentibus, unice imperator.

LV

Oramus, si forte non molestumst,
demonstres ubi sint tuae tenebrae.
te campo quaesivimus minore,
te in circo, te in omnibus libellis,
te in templo summi Iovis sacrato;
in Magni simul ambulatione
femellas omnes, amice, prendi,
quas vultu vidi tamen sereno.
a, vel te sic ipse flagitabam,
"Camerium mihi, pessimae puellae!"
quaedam inquit, nudum reducta pectus,
"em hic in roseis latet papillis."
sed te iam ferre Herculi labos est.
non custos si fingar ille Cretum,
non si Pegaseo ferar volatu,
non Ladas ego pinnipesve Perseus,
non Rhesi niveae citaeque bigae:
adde huc plumipedas volatilesque,
ventorumque simul require cursum;
quos iunctos, Cameri, mihi dicares,
defessus tamen omnibus medullis
et multis langoribus peresus
essem te, mi amice, quaeritando.
tanto ten fastu negas, amice?
dic nobis ubi sis futurus, ede
audacter, committe, crede luci.

LIVa

Again you will be angry at my iambics,
Harmless although they are, my one and only general.

LV

Perhaps, if it is not a nuisance to you,
You would be good enough to tell me where you are hiding.
I have looked for you in the lesser Campus,
In the circus, and among the lost property;
I have looked for you in the temple of Jove
And in Pompey's walk
I stopped all the women and asked them
But they looked at me with the utmost innocence.
These are the women I begged:
'Give me Camerius, you indelicate girls.'
One of them said, pulling open her dress:
'He is here, somewhere between my nipples.'
Really it is a labour of Hercules to put up with you.
If I were as mobile as the giant of Crete
Or could fly through the air after the manner of Pegasus,
If I were Ladas, or Perseus with wings on his feet
Or the while horses of Rhesus;
You may name all the feather-footed and volatile
And at the same time invoke the course of the winds.
But, Camerius, though you produce the whole lot
My bones would ache, I should suffer repeated fainting fits
Before I succeeded in laying hands on you.
Why do you keep yourself from me? It is insolent.
Tell me where you expect to be. Give over,
Be brave, make up your mind, tell the news.

num te lacteolae tenent puellae?
si linguam clauso tenes in ore,
fructus proicies amoris omnes:
verbosa gaudet Venus loquella.
vel si vis, licet obseres palatum,
dum vestri sim particeps amoris.

LVI

O rem ridiculam, Cato, et iocosam
dignamque auribus et tuo cachinno.
ride, quicquid amas, Cato, Catullum:
res est ridicula et nimis iocosa.
deprendi modo pupulum puellae
crustantem: hunc ego, si placet Dionae,
pro telo rigida mea cecidi.

LVII

Pulcre convenit improbis cinaedis,
Mamurrae pathicoque Caesarique.
nec mirum: maculae pares utrisque,
urbana altera et illa Formiana,
impressae resident nec eluentur:
morbosi pariter, gemelli utrique,
uno in lecticulo erudituli ambo,
non hic quam ille magis vorax adulter,
rivales socii puellularum.
pulcre convenit improbis cinaedis.

Have those sleek girls got you?
If you keep your face shut and say nothing
You are losing all the pleasure you had from them.
Venus likes to be talked about.
Still keep quiet if you must, but on one condition
That you give me a share of whatever it is you have found.

LVI

Cato, I will tell you a funny thing
Worthy of your ears and loud cackle;
Laugh, as much as you love Catullus, Cato:
The thing is ridiculous, really too funny.
I caught a small boy jogging a girl
So, love forgive me,
I set about him with my rigid rod.

LVII

They suit one another well enough
The pathic Mamurra and the pathic Caesar.
The stains in them are about equal,
One from the city and one from Formiae,
And in neither will they ever be washed out:
Both alike sick, both lying on one bed,
A pair of twins, both of them even writers
You could not say one was more adulterous than the other.
They fight over little girls and then share them.
They certainly suit one another well enough.

LVIII

Caeli, Lesbia nostra, Lesbia illa,
illa Lesbia, quam Catullus unam
plus quam se atque suos amavit omnes,
nunc in quadriviis et angiportis
glubit magnanimi Remi nepotes.

LIX

Bononiensis Rufa Rufulum fellat
uxor Meneni, saepe quam in sepulcretis
vidistis ipso rapere de rogo cenam,
cum devolutum ex igne prosequens panem
ab semiraso tunderetur ustore.

LX

Num te leaena montibus Libystinis
aut Scylla latrans infima inguinum parte
tam mente dura procreavit ac taetra,
ut supplicis vocem in novissimo casu
contemptam haberes, a nimis fero corde?

LVIII

Caelius, our Lesbia, Lesbia, that Lesbia
More loved by Catullus than any besides
—More than he loves himself and his pleasures—
Is now, in the alleyways and even at crossroads
Fucked by the noble sons of the Romans.

LIX

Rufa of Bononia sucks Rufulus?
The wife of Menenius, whom you have seen in the graveyards
Snatching her supper from the funeral pyre?
—She would run after a loaf as it rolled down out of the flames
And be thumped for it by the half-shaven undertaker's assistant.

LX

Did a lioness from the Libyan mountains
Or Scylla barking out of the mouth of her womb
Give birth to you? You are so hard and inhuman.
Your suppliants' voice crying in its last need
You treat with contempt, so very cruel is your heart.

LXI

Collis o Heliconii
cultor, Uraniae genus,
qui rapis teneram ad virum
virginem, o Hymenaee Hymen,
o Hymen Hymenaee,

cinge tempora floribus
suave olentis amaraci,
flammeum cape, laetus huc
huc veni niveo gerens
luteum pede soccum,

excitusque hilari die,
nuptialia concinens
voce carmina tinnula,
pelle humum pedibus, manu
pineam quate taedam.

namque Iunia Manlio,
qualis Idalium colens
venit ad Phrygium Venus
iudicem, bona cum bona
nubet alite virgo,

floridis velut enitens
myrtus Asia ramulis,
quos Hamadryades deae
ludicrum sibi roscido
nutriunt umore.

quare age huc aditum ferens
perge linquere Thespiae
rupis Aonios specus,
nympha quos super irrigat
frigerans Aganippe,

LXI

Sprung from Urania
You inhabit Helicon;
Young girls you carry off
To men, O Hymenaeus,
O Hymen Hymenaeus.

Put flowers in your hair,
Sweet smelling marjoram,
Put on a veil and come,
Happy, with yellow shoes
On your white feet.

Excited on this day,
Sing all the wedding songs
At the top of your voice;
Dance, and jump about,
A pine torch in your hand.

Vinia is marrying Manlius;
Like Venus from Idalium
She comes to have her beauty judged.
She is a good girl and
The omens are good.

Like the Asian myrtle,
All her branches shining
As if the Hamadryads
Had poured their dew upon her
To amuse themselves.

So make your approach,
Leaving without delay
The caves in the Thespian rock
Which Aganippe waters
Coldly from above.

ac domum dominam voca
coniugis cupidam novi,
mentem amore revinciens,
ut tenax edera huc et huc
arborem implicat errans.

vosque item simul, integrae
virgines, quibus advenit
par dies, agite in modum
dicite "o Hymenaee Hymen,
o Hymen Hymenaee."

ut lubentius, audiens
se citarier ad suum
munus, huc aditum ferat
dux bonae Veneris, boni
coniugator amoris.

quis deus magis est ama-
tis petendus amantibus?
quem colent homines magis
caelitum? o Hymenaee Hymen,
o Hymen Hymenaee.

te suis tremulus parens
invocat, tibi virgines
zonula soluunt sinus,
te timens cupida novus
captat aure maritus.

tu fero iuveni in manus
floridam ipse puellulam
dedis a gremio suae
matris, o Hymenaee Hymen,
o Hymen Hymenaee.

And call the lady home.
She, wanting her new husband,
Tangles her mind with love
As the persistent ivy here and there
    Clings vaguely to a tree.

You with me too, you girls
Whose turn is coming;
Take up the chant together with
O Hymenaeus Hymen,
    O Hymen Hymenaeus.

Hearing himself so called
No doubt he'll come more gladly
To do his part which is
In turn to bring in Venus:
    He connects up the love.

What god should be more sought
By those who love and are loved?
What god is there more worshipped?
O Hymenaeus Hymen,
    O Hymen Hymenaeus.

The tremulous old man
Calls on you for his children:
The girls take off their clothes:
The bridegroom in a dither
    Listens for your approach.

To the wild youth you hand over
The girl who is just florescent
Straight from the arms of mother
O Hymenaeus Hymen,
    O Hymen Hymenaeus.

nil potest sine te Venus,
fama quod bona comprobet,
commodi capere: at potest
te volente. quis huic deo
    compararier ausit?

nulla quit sine te domus
liberos dare, nec parens
stirpe nitier: at potest
te volente. quis huic deo
    compararier ausit?

quae tuis careat sacris,
non queat dare praesides
terra finibus: at queat
te volente. quis huic deo
    compararier ausit?

claustra pandite ianuae,
virgo adest. viden ut faces
splendidas quatiunt comas?
* * *
tardet ingenuus pudor:
* * *
quem tamen magis audiens
    flet, quod ire necesse est.

flere desine. non tibi, Aurunculeia, periculumst,
nequa femina pulcrior
clarum ab Oceano diem
    viderit venientem.

Venus can do nothing without you,
That is, nothing respectable;
She can get nothing out of it: but with you
She can. No one should dare
          To compare himself with you.

Without you no house can have children
No father can see the succession
Continued: but with you
He can. So no one should dare
          To compare himself to you.

A country without your rites
Will find no protectors
To stand at the frontiers: but with you
It will. So no one should dare
          To compare himself to you.

Open the door, she is coming
And in she comes, the torches
Shake their hair

* * *

But shyness holds her back.

* * *

Preferring to listen to this
          She cries because she must go.

Do not cry. There is no danger
For you, Aurunculeia,
That any more beautiful woman
Will see the clear day rising
          Out of the sea.

talis in vario solet
divitis domini hortulo
stare flos hyancinthinus.
sed moraris, abit dies:
prodeas, nova nupta.

prodeas, nova nupta, si
iam videtur, et audias
nostra verba. vide ut faces
aureas quatiunt comas:
prodeas, nova nupta.

non tuus levis in mala
deditus vir adultera
probra turpia persequens
a tuis teneris volet
secubare papillis.

lenta sed velut adsitas
vitis implicat arbores.
implicabitur in tuum
complexum. sed abit dies:
prodeas, nova nupta.

o cubile, quod omnibus

* * *
* * *
* * *

candido pede lecti,

quae tuo veniunt ero,
quanta gaudia, quae vaga
nocte, quae medio die
gaudeat! sed abit dies:
prodeas, nova nupta.

In the varied garden
Of the expensive householder
The hyacinth stands so.
You waste time, day is going:
Bride, come out.

Bride, come out! If you can bear to,
At long last, if you can hear us;
We are speaking. Come out and see
The torches shake their hair:
Bride, come out.

Your man will not be flippant
And, giving himself over
To mean adulteries,
Want to lie elsewhere than
Between your gentle breasts.

But as the vine embraces
A tree that's planted near it
So he will be entangled
In your embrace. The day goes:
Bride, come out.

O bed, which everyone

* * *

* * *

* * *

White foot in bed

How glad your man will be
In the passing night, how glad
He will be, in the afternoon!
And yet, this day runs out:
Bride, come out.

tollite, o pueri, faces:
flammeum video venire.
ite, concinite in modum
"io Hymen Hymenaee io,
io Hymen Hymenaee."

ne diu taceat procax
Fescennina iocatio,
neu nuces pueris peget
desertum domini audiens
concubinus amorem.

da nuces pueris, iners
concubine: satis diu
lusisti nucibus: lubet
iam servire Talasio.
concubine, nuces da.

sordebant tibi vilicae,
concubine, hodie atque heri:
nunc tuum cinerarius
tondet os. miser a miser
concubine, nuces da.

diceris male te a tuis
unguentate glabris, marite,
abstinere: sed abstine.
io Hymen Hymenaee io,
io Hymen Hymenaee.

scimus haec tibi quae licent
sola cognita: sed marito
ista non eadem licent.
io Hymen Hymenaee io,
io Hymen Hymenaee.

Boys, lift the torches up:
I see the bridal veil.
Go, chant together now:
Io Hymen, Hymen Io,
        Io Hymen Hymenaeus.

Do not prohibit now
The Fescinnine impertinences;
And let the boys have nuts.
The boy that went to bed
        With Manlius, gives them out.

You pansy boy, give nuts;
You've played nuts long enough
And now your time has come
To serve Talassius:
        You pansy boy, give nuts.

And only yesterday
The country girls seemed nothing!
But now you get a shave;
Hard luck, you pansy boy,
        Hard luck, but give the nuts.

Seeing the bridegroom oiled
And combed, one wonders, can
He leave the slippery boys?
But leave them. Io Hymen,
        Io Hymen Hymenaeus.

We know what you allowed
Yourself, was once allowed,
But husbands are not free.
Io Hymen, Hymenaeus Io,
        Io Hymen Hymenaeus.

nupta, tu quoque, quae tuus
vir petet, cave ne neges,
ni petitum aliunde est.
io Hymen Hymenaee io,
        io Hymen Hymenaee.

en tibi domus ut potens
et beata viri tui,
quae tibi sine serviat
io Hymen Hymenaee io,
        io Hymen Hymenaee,

usque dum tremulum movens
cana tempus anilitas
omnia omnibus annuit.
io Hymen Hymenaee io,
        io Hymen Hymenaee.

transfer omine cum bono
limen aureolos pedes,
rasilemque subi forem.
io Hymen Hymenaee io,
        io Hymen Hymenaee.

aspice, intus ut accubans
vir tuus Tyrio in toro
totus immineat tibi.
io Hymen Hymenaee io,
        io Hymen Hymenaee.

illi non minus ac tibi
pectore uritur intimo
flamma, sed penite magis.
io Hymen Hymenaee io,
        io Hymen Hymenaee.

And bride, be sure you give
Your husband all he asks
Or he will go elsewhere.
Io Hymen Hymenaeus Io,
        Io Hymen Hymenaeus.

This is the house, a large
And pleasant one; it's his
And it will serve for you
(Io Hymen Hymenaeus Io,
        Io Hymen Hymenaeus).

Until extreme old age
Forces your head to nod
Assent to everything.
Io Hymen Hymenaeus Io,
        Io Hymen Hymenaeus.

And with good omen now
Carry your golden feet
Across the threshold, through
The polished doorway. Io,
        Io Hymen Hymenaeus.

Inside, your husband rests
Upon a Tyrian couch,
His mind intent on you.
Io Hymen Hymenaeus Io,
        Io Hymen Hymenaeus.

The fire burns in his heart
As much as in your own
But deeper, certainly.
Io Hymen Hymenaeus Io,
        Io Hymen Hymenaeus.

mitte bracchiolum teres,
praetextate, puellulae:
iam cubile adeat viri.
io Hymen Hymenaee io,
io Hymen Hymenaee.

vos bonae senibus viris
cognitae bene feminae,
collocate puellulam.
io Hymen Hymenaee io,
io Hymen Hymenaee.

iam licet venias, marite:
uxor in thalamo tibist
ore floridulo nitens,
alba parthenice velut
luteumve papaver.

at, marite, (ita me iuvent
caelites) nihilo minus
pulcher es, neque te Venus
neglegit. sed abit dies:
perge, ne remorare.

non diu remoratus es,
iam venis. bona te Venus
iuverit, quoniam palam
quod cupis capis et bonum
non abscondis amorem.

ille pulveris Africi
siderumque micantium
subducat numerum prius,
qui vostri numerare vult
multa milia ludi.

The child who leads the girl
Lets go her slender arm;
Go to your husband's bed.
Io Hymen Hymenaeus Io,
          Io Hymen Hymenaeus.

You married women now
Whose husbands have grown old
Put the girl in her place.
Io Hymen Hymenaeus Io,
          Io Hymen Hymenaeus.

Now, bridegroom, you may come;
Your wife is in the bed,
Her face shines like a flower,
Like a white daisy or
          A golden poppy.

Husband (so help me gods)
You are as beautiful.
Venus did not forget
You either. The day goes;
          Go on, and lose no time.

You lose none; here you come.
Kind Venus help you since
You now so openly
Take what you want
          And do not hide your love.

You could more quickly count
The sands of Africa
Or the glittering stars
Than find the total of
          Your many thousand games.

ludite ut lubet, et brevi
liberos date. non decet
tam vetus sine liberis
nomen esse, sed indidem
          semper ingenerari.

Torquatus volo parvulus
matris e gremio suae
porrigens teneras manus
dulce rideat ad patrem
          semihiante labello.

sit suo similis patri
Manlio et facile insciis
noscitetur ab omnibus
et pudicitiam suae
          matris indicet ore.

talis illius a bona
matre laus genus approbet,
qualis unica ab optima
matre Telemacho manet
          fama Penelopeo.

claudite ostia, virgines:
lusimus satis. at, boni
coniuges, bene vivite et
munere assiduo valentem
          exercete iuventam.

Play as you will and soon
Produce a child. A name
As old as yours must not
Be left without an heir;
          The tree must fruit.

A baby Torquatus
I want, at his mother's breast,
Stretching his tender hands
Towards his father, and smiling
          With half-parted lips.

May he be so like
His father Manlius
That the instant he appears
Nobody will doubt where
          His mother got him from.

May his name be as good
As now his mother's is
So from Penelope
Telemachus derived
          And left, a noble fame.

Girls, close the door. For we
Have played enough. But you,
The married pair, good luck;
Play out assiduously
          Your vigorous youth.

LXII

Iuvenes

Vesper adest, iuvenes, consurgite: Vepser Olympo
expectata diu vix tandem lumina tollit.
surgere iam tempus, iam pinguis linquere mensas;
iam veniet virgo, iam dicetur Hymenaeus.
Hymen o Hymenaee, Hymen ades o Hymenaee!

Puellae

cernitis, innuptae, iuvenes? consurgite contra;
nimirum Oetaeos ostendit Noctifer ignes.
sic certest; viden ut perniciter exiluere?
non temere exiluere, canent quod visere par est.
Hymen o Hymenaee, Hymen ades o Hymenaee!

Iuvenes

non facilis nobis, aequales, palma paratast;
aspicite, innuptae secum ut meditata requirunt.
non frustra meditantur, habent memorabile quod sit.
nec mirum, penitus quae tota mente laborent.
nos alio mentes, alio divisimus aures;
iure igitur vincemur; amat victoria curam.
quare nunc animos saltem committite vestros;
dicere iam incipient, iam respondere decebit.
Hymen o Hymenaee, Hymen ades o Hymenaee!

Puellae

Hespere, qui caelo fertur crudelior ignis?
qui natam possis complexu avellere matris,
complexu matris retinentem avellere natam,
et iuveni ardenti castam donare puellam.

LXII

Young men

Evening is here, young men. Stand up and look. From Olympus
Vesper at last has raised the light you awaited so long.
It is time to get up from the couch and the luxurious tables.
The bride is now coming in, the prayers of Hymen are said.
        Hymen O Hymenaeus, approach Hymenaeus.

Girls

Girls, do you see the young men? Let us stand up and face them;
Surely the Star of Night shows its Oetaean fires.
That for sure; do you see how dangerously they have jumped up?
It was not for fun; they will sing; there'll be something to watch.
        Hymen O Hymenaeus, approach Hymenaeus.

Young men

It is not easy for us, the young men, to win the prize:
Look, the girls are going over the part that they have learnt.
They are not doing that for nothing; what they've learnt is a thing to remember;
No wonder they turn it over so deep in their minds.
What we learnt went in at one ear and out at the other:
Serve us right, we shall be beaten; to win you've got to attend.
At least let us try to see if our brains are as good as theirs:
Already they've started to speak; it will be good for us to reply.
        Hymen O Hymenaeus, approach Hymenaeus.

Girls

Hesperus, what crueller star than you is there up in the sky?
You don't mind taking girls away from their mothers?
Taking a girl away when she's holding tight to her mother?
And giving a girl that is chaste to an ardent young man?

quid faciunt hostes capta crudelius urbe?
Hymen o Hymenaee, Hymen ades o Hymenaee!

Iuvenes

Hespere, qui caelo lucet iucundior ignis?
qui desponsa tua firmes conubia flamma,
quae pepigere viri, pepigerunt ante parentes,
nec iunxere prius quam se tuus extulit ardor.
quid datur a divis felici optatius hora?
Hymen o Hymenaee, Hymen ades o Hymenaee!

Puellae

Hesperus e nobis, aequales, abstulit unam
* * *

Iuvenes

namque tuo adventu vigilat custodia semper.
nocte latent fures, quos idem saepe revertens.
Hespere, mutato comprendis nomine Eous.
* * *

at lubet innuptis ficto te carpere questu.
quid tum, si carpunt, tacita quem mente requirunt?
Hymen o Hymenaee, Hymen ades o Hymenaee!

Puellae

ut flos in saeptis secretus nascitur hortis,
ignotus pecori, nullo convulsus aratro,
quem mulcent aurae, firmat sol, educat imber,
* * *

multi illum pueri, multae optavere puellae:
idem cum tenui carptus defloruit ungui,
nulli illum pueri, nullae optavere puellae:

Do the enemy soldiers do worse when they capture a town?
Hymen O Hymenaeus, approach Hymenaeus.

Young men

Hesperus, what pleasanter star than you is there in the sky?
You are the one who sees that the promise comes true,
The contracts the bridegroom has made, and the families before that,
Cannot be carried out until your fire is up.
Is there any time the gods give which is an improvement on this?
Hymen O Hymenaeus, approach Hymenaeus.

Girls

Hesperus has taken one of us girls away
* * *

Young men

When you come up the watch-dogs are always let off the chain
For thieves can hide in the night, and you often find them out
When you go back in the morning, having changed your name to Eous.
* * *

The girls complain about you but we don't believe a word;
We know that, if they complain, they want you all the same.
Hymen O Hymenaeus, approach Hymenaeus.

Girls

As a flower springs up unknown behind a garden wall
Where the beast can't eat it and it can't be convulsed by a plough.
The breezes stroke it, the sun makes it stronger, the rain brings it on
* * *

Many boys would like to have it, and many girls would too.
Once torn up by sharp nails, it loses its flower,
Then no boys want it, and no girls want it either:

sic virgo dum intacta manet, dum cara suis est;
cum castum amisit polluto corpore florem,
nec pueris iucunda manet nec cara puellis.
Hymen o Hymenaee, Hymen ades o Hymenaee!

Iuvenes

ut vidua in nudo vitis quae nascitur arvo
numquam se extollit, numquam mitem educat uvam
sed tenerum prono deflectens pondere corpus
iam iam contingit summum radice flagellum;
hanc nulli agricolae, nulli coluere iuvenci.
at si forte eademst ulmo coniuncta marita,
multi illam agricolae, multi coluere iuvenci:
sic virgo dum intacta manet, dum inculta senescit;
cum par conubium maturo tempore adeptast,
cara viro magis et minus est invisa parenti.
Hymen o Hymenaee, Hymen ades o Hymenaee!

et tu ne pugna cum tali coniuge, virgo.
non aequumst pugnare, pater cui tradidit ipse,
ipse pater cum matre, quibus parere necessest.
virginitas non tota tuast, ex parte parentumst;
tertia pars patrist, pars est data tertia matri,
tertia sola tuast: noli pugnare duobus,
qui genero sua iura simul cum dote dederunt.
Hymen o Hymenaee, Hymen ades o Hymenaee!

While a girl remains chaste, her family are fond of her
But if she loses her flower, her body is not so nice;
She finds she's no catch for the boys and even her girl friends go.
Hymen O Hymenaeus, approach Hymenaeus.

Young men

As a vine which grows on its own in the open field
Never climbs at all, or produces a decent grape
But its tender body bends with its own dead weight
So that the top of it practically touches the root
No farmer comes near it, no oxen plough up the ground.
But if it happens to find a tree to support it
Many farmers will care for it, many oxen will plough.
So a girl, as long as she's virgin, grows old in neglect
But when she is suited in time with the right sort of marriage
She is dear to a man, and not such a trial to her family.
Hymen O Hymenaeus, approach Hymenaeus.

So, girl, it is really not wise to resist such a husband.
You should not resist, since your father has given you away;
Your mother and father decided, you should do as they tell you.
Virginity isn't just yours, it is partly your parents' as well.
A third is your father's, a third is your mother's, a third is your own.
That is all you have. Better not resist the two others.
They have given their rights with the dowry, and you go with that.
Hymen O Hymenaeus, approach Hymenaeus.

LXIII

Super alta vectus Attis celeri rate maria
Phrygium ut nemus citato cupide pede tetigit
adiitque opaca silvis redimita loca deae,
stimulatus ibi furenti rabie, vague anima,
devolvit ili acuto sibi pondera silece.
itaque ut relicta sensit sibi membra sine viro,
etiam recente terrae sola sanguine maculans
niveis citata cepit manibus leve typanum,
typanum tuom, Cybebe, tua, Mater, initia.
quatiensque terga tauri teneris cava digitis
canere haec suis adortast tremebunda comitibus.
"agite ite ad alta, Gallae, Cybeles nemora simul,
simul ite, Dindymenae dominae vaga pecora,
aliena quae petentes velut exules loca celeri
sectam meam executae duce me mihi comites
rapidum salum tulistis truculentaque pelage
et corpus evirastis Veneris nimio odio,
hilarate erae citatis erroribus animum.
mora tarda mente cedat; simul ite, sequimini
Phrygiam ad domum Cybebes, Phrygia ad nemora deae,
ubi cymbalum sonat vox, ubi tympana reboant,
tibicen ubi canit Phryx curvo grave calamo,
ubi capita Maenades vi iaciunt ederigerae,
ubi sacra sancta acutis ululatibus agitant,
ubi suevit illa divae volitare vaga cohors:
quo nos decet citatis celerare tripudiis."
Simul haec comitibus Attis cecinit notha mulier.
thiasus repente linguis trepidantibus ulalat,
leve tympanum remugit, cava cymbala recrepant,
viridem citus adit Idam properante pede chorus.
furibunda simul anhelans vaga vadit, animama gens,
comitata tympano Attis per opaca nemora dux,
veluti iuvenca vitans onus indomita iugi:

LXIII

Carried in a fast ship over profound seas
Attis, eager and hurried, reached the Phrygian grove,
The goddess's dark places, crowned with woodland.
And there, exalted by amorous rage, his mind gone,
He cut off his testicles with a sharp flint.
She then, aware of her limbs without the man,
While the ground was still spotted with fresh blood
Quickly took in her snowy hands a tambourine
Such as serves your initiates, Cybele, instead of a trumpet
And, shaking the hollow calf-hide with delicate fingers.
Quivering, she began to sing to the troop this:
'Go together, votaresses, to the high groves of Cybele.
Go together, wandering herd of the lady of Dindymus.
Quick into exile, you looked for foreign places
And, following me and the rule I had adopted,
You bore with the salt tide and the violence of the high sea
And emasculated your bodies from too much hatred of Venus:
Delight the lady's mind with your errant haste.
Overcome your reluctance: together
Go to the Phrygian shrine of Cybele, to her groves
Where the voice of cymbals sounds, the tambourines rattle,
Where the Phrygian piper sings with the deep curved pipe,
Where Maenads wearing ivy throw back their heads,
Where they practice the sacred rites with sharp yells.
Where they flutter around the goddess's cohort:
It is there we must go with our rapid dances.'
As Attis, the counterfeit woman, sang this to her companions,
The choir howled suddenly with tumultuous tongues.
The tambourine bellows, the cymbals clash again;
The swift troop moves off to Ida with hurrying feet.
Crazy, panting, drifting, at her last gasp,
Attis with her tambourine leads them through the opaque groves
Like an unbroken heifer refusing the yoke:

rapidae ducem sequuntur Gallae properipedem.
itaque ut domum Cybebes tetigere lassulae,
nimio e labore somnum capiunt sine Cerere.
piger his labante langore oculos sopor operit:
abit in quiete molli rabidus furor animi.
sed ubi oris aurei Sol radiantibus oculis
lustravit aethera album, sola dura, mare ferum,
pepulitque noctis umbras vegetis sonipedibus,
ibi Somnus excitum Attin fugiens citus abiit:
trepidante eum recepit dea Pasithea sinu.
ita de quiete molli rapida sine rabie
simul ipse pectore Attis sua facta recoluit,
liquidaque mente vidit sine quis ubique foret,
animo aestuante rusum reditum ad vada tetulit.
ibi maria vasta visens lacrimantibus oculis,
patriam allocuta maestast ita voce miseriter.

"Patria o mei creatrix, patria o mea genetrix,
ego quam miser relinquens, dominos ut erifugae
famuli solent, ad Idae tetuli nemora pedem,
ut apud nivem et ferarum gelida stabula forem
et earum omnia adirem furibunda latibula,
ubinam aut quibus locis te positam, patria, reor?
cupit ipsa pupula ad te sibi derigere aciem,
rabie fera carens dum breve tempus animus est.
egone a mea remota haec ferar in nemora domo?
patria, bonis, amicis, genitoribus abero?
abero foro, palaestra, stadio et guminasiis?
miser a miser, querendumst etiam atque etiam, anime
quod enim, genus figuraest, ego non quod habuerim?
ego mulier, ego adolescens, ego ephebus, ego puer,
ego guminasi fui flos, ego eram decus olei:
mihi ianuae frequentes, mihi limina tepida,
mihi floridis corollis redimita domus erat,
linquendum ubi esset orto mihi sole cubiculum.
ego nunc deum ministra et Cybeles famula ferar?

The swift votaresses follow their swift-footed leader.
When they reach Cybele's shrine they are feeble and worn.
Sleep covers their eyes with a heavy blanket;
Their rabid madness subsides to a girlish quiet.
But when the golden sun with his streaming eyes
Purified the white sky, hard land, wild sea,
And drove away the shadows of night with his thundering horses,
Attis was aroused and Sleep went quickly from her
Back to the trembling arms of the goddess Pasithea.
Then from her girlish quiet, with no hurrying madness,
Attis remembered what she had done
And saw in her lucid mind what was missing and where she was.
Tempestuously she turned back to the shore.
There, looking at the open sea with tearful eyes,
With grief in her voice she addressed her native land:
'Land which begot me, land which brought me forth,
I am abject to abandon you like a runaway slave.
My feet have carried me to the groves of Ida
To be among snow in the cold lairs of wild beasts;
I shall visit their violent haunts.
Where, O my land, can I imagine you are?
My eye desires you and narrows as it turns towards you
In this short interval when my mind is unfrenzied.
Shall I be carried to the forests, from my far-off home?
Away from country, goods, friends, family?
From the Forum, palaestra, racecourse and gymnasium?
There is nothing for me but misery.
What shape is there that I have not had?
A woman now, I have been man, youth and boy;
I was athlete, the wrestler.
There were crowds round my door, my fans slept on the doorstep;
There were flowers all over the house
When I left my bed at sunrise.
Shall I be a waiting maid to the gods, the slave of Cybele?

ego Maenas, ego mei pars, ego vir sterilis ero?
ego viridis algida Idae nive amicta loca colam?
ego vitam agam sub altis Phrygiae columinibus
ubi cerva silvicultrix, ubi aper nemorivagus?
iam iam dolet quod egi, iam iamque paenitet."

Roseis ut hic labellis sonitus citus abiit,
geminas deorum ad aures nova nuntia referens,
ibi iuncta iuga resolvens Cybele leonibus
laevumque pecoris hostem stimulans ita loquitur.
"agedum" inquit "age feroxi, fac ut hunc furor agitet,
fac uti furoris ictu reditum in nemora ferat,
mea libere nimis qui fugere imperia cupit
age caede terga cauda, tua verbera patere,
fac cuncta mugienti fremitu loca retonent,
rutilam ferox torosa cervice quate iubam."
ait haec minax Cybelle religatque iuga manu.
ferus ipse sese adhortans rapidum incitat animo,
vadit, fremit, refringit virgulta pede vago.
at ubi umida albicantis loca litoris adiit,
tenerumque vidit Attin prope marmora pelagi,
facit impetum: ille demens fugit in nemora fera:
ibi semper omne vitae spatium famula fuit.

Dea magna, dea Cybebe, dea domina Dindymi,
procul a mea tuus sit furor omnis, era, domo:
alios age incitatos, alios age rabidos.

LXIV

Peliaco quondam prognatae vertice pinus
dicuntur liquidas Neptuni nasse per undas
Phasidos ad fluctus et fines Aeeteos,
cum lecti iuvenes, Argivae robora pubis,
auratam optantes Colchis avertere pellem

I a Maenad, I a part of myself, I impotent?
Shall I live above the snow line on green Ida?
Shall I pass my life under the rocky peaks of Phrygia
Where the doe runs in the woods, where the boar mooches in the glade?
I regret now, now, what I have done, I repent of it, now!'
As these words hurried away from her pink lips,
Bringing a new message to the ears of the gods,
Cybele, letting her lions off the leash
And urging forward the beast on the left hand,
Said: 'Get on, be fierce, see that he's driven mad;
Make him insane enough to return to the forest;
He has had the impertinence to want to be out of my power.
Come on, lash around with your tail till you hurt yourself:
Make the whole neighborhood ring with your bellowing roar.
Be fierce, shake the red mane on your muscular neck.'
Thus the threatening Cybele, and she wound the leash round her hand
The beast stirs up his courage and rouses himself to fury.
He is off, he roars, he breaks up the undergrowth.
When he came to the wet sand on the whitening shore
He charged: Attis, mad, flew into the wild woods:
There, for the rest of her life, she lived as a slave.
Great Goddess, Goddess Cybele, Goddess lady of Dindymus,
May all your fury be far from my house.
Incite the others, go. Drive other men mad.

LXIV

Pines from the summit of Pelion,
It is said, floated in the running seas
As far as Phasis and the shores of Aeetes
When elect youths, the pick of Argive manhood,
Seeking to relieve the Colchians of the golden fleece,

ausi sunt vada salsa cita decurrere puppi,
caerula verrentes abiegnis aequora palmis;
diva quibus retinens in summis urbibus arces
ipsa levi fecit volitantem flamine currum,
pinea coniungens inflexae texta carinae.
illa rudem cursu prima imbuit Amphitriten.

Quae simul ac rostro ventosum proscidit aequor,
tortaque remigio spumis incanduit unda,
emersere freti candenti e gurgite vultus
aequoreae monstrum Nereides admirantes.
illa atque alia viderunt luce marinas
mortales oculis nudato corpore Nymphas
nutricum tenus extantis e gurgite cano.
tum Thetidis Peleus incensus fertur amore,
tum Thetis humanos non despexit hymenaeos,
tum Thetidi pater ipse iugandum Pelea sensit.
o nimis optato saeclorum tempore nati
heroes, salvete, deum gens o bona matrum
progenies salvete it iterum
vos ego saepe meo vos carmine compellabo:
teque adeo eximie taedis felicibus aucte,
Thessaliae columen Peleu, cui Iuppiter ipse,
ipse suos divum genitor concessit amores.
tene Thetis tenuit pulcherrima Nereine?
tene suam Tethys concessit ducere neptem,
Oceanusque, mari totum qui amplectitur orbem?

Quis simul optatae finito tempore luces
advenere, domum conventu tota frequentat
Thessalia, oppletar laetanti regia coetu:
dona ferunt prae se, declarant gaudia vultu.
deseritur Cieros, linquunt Phthiotica Tempe
Crannonisque domos ac moenia Larisaea,
Pharsalum coeunt, Pharsalia tecta frequentant.
rura colit nemo, mollescunt colla iuvencis,
non humilis curvis purgatur vinea rastris,

Had the courage to run over salt waves with a rapid craft,
Sweeping the blue deep with pinewood oar-blades;
The goddess who keeps the city fortress-tops
Herself devised this chariot which would fly with the wind,
Joining the pinewood structure to a bending keel.
It was the first ship that attempted a voyage.
As soon as the prow cut through the windy sea
And the waves whitened as the rowing churned them up
The Nereids came out of the whiteness,
Amazed at this new form of marine animal.
On that day at least mortals did really see
Naked sea-nymphs sticking out of the water showing their tits.
It is supposed to have been then that Peleus became mad about Thetis,
That Thetis decided she wouldn't despise human marriage
And that the Father admitted to himself that Peleus would have to have her.
O heroes, born in that most happy age,
I salute you, race of the gods, I salute you
O excellent offspring of excellent mothers.
I shall often address you in the course of my song:
And you, notably multiplied by fortunate marriage torches,
The pillar of Thessaly, Peleus, on whom Jupiter himself,
Who begot the gods, bestowed his love:
Did Thetis embrace you? She was the most beautiful of the Nereids.
Did Tethys allow you to marry her granddaughter,
And Oceanus, who wraps up the whole world in the sea?
At last the waiting was at an end and the day came.
All Thessaly poured into the house;
They come in, presents first, and wear looks of rejoicing.
Cieros is deserted; they leave Phthiotic Tempe,
The houses round Crannon and the walls of Larissa,
And crowd indoors at Pharsalus.
Nobody works on the land, the oxen go soft round the neck,
The vine is left straggling and the hoeing isn't done.

non falx attenuat frondatorum arboris umbram,
non glaebam prono convellit vomere taurus,
squalida desertis rubigo infertur aratris.

Ipsius at sedes, quacumque opulenta recessit
regia, fulgenti splendent auro atque argento.
candet ebur soliis, collucent opcula mensae,
tota domus gaudet regali splendida gaza.
pulvinar vero divae geniale locatur
sedibus in mediis, Indo quod dente politum
tincta tegit roseo conchyli purpura fuco.
Haec vestis priscis hominum variata figuris
heroum mira virtutes indicat arte.
namque fluentisono prospectans litore Diae
Thesea cedentem celeri cum classe tuetur
indomitos in corde gerens Ariadna furores;
necdum etiam sese quae visit visere credit,
ut pote fallaci quae tum primum excita somno
desertam in sola miseram se cernat harena.
immemor at iuvenis fugiens pellit vada remis,
irrita ventosae linquens promissa procellae.
Quem procul ex alga maestis Minois ocellis
saxea ut effigies bacchantis prospicit, eheu,
prospicit et magnis curarum fluctuat undis,
non flavo retinens subtilem vertice mitram,
non contecta levi velatum pectus amictu,
non tereti strophio lactentis vincta papillas,
omnia quae toto delapsa e corpore passim
ipsius ante pedes fluctus salis adludebant.
sed neque tum mitrae neque tum fluitantis amictus
illa vicem curans toto ex te pectore, Theseu,
toto animo, tota pendebat perdita mente.
a misera, assiduis quam luctibus externavit
spinosas Erycina serens in pectore curas
illa tempestate, ferox quo tempore Theseus

The pruning hook has a holiday and the trees grow thick;
The ox stops dragging the ploughshare through lumps of earth
And rust begins to develop on the deserted equipment.

But Peleus's house, as far as you can see inside that millionaire palace,
Shines brilliantly with every kind of gold and silver.
The seats are of ivory, and the cups on the table gleam.
The whole house is gay with splendid paraphernalia.
In a central position is the golden bed,
Polished elephant tusk, with the hangings dyed purple with shell dye.
The bedspread, worked with figures from former times,
Illustrating the deeds of the heroes, is a remarkable production:
Ariadne, looking out from the wave-beaten shore,
Sees Theseus disappearing with his rapid boats.
She has fury in her heart and cannot believe her eyes,
For awakened at last from deceptive sleep
She sees herself miserably alone on the lonely sand.
But the youth is in flight and the oars fall in time on the water;
He leaves his empty promises to the winds and squalls.
From among the seaweed the daughter of Minos
With tears in her eyes looks out like a stone bacchanal.
She looks out, alas, washed by great waves of care,
Not keeping her fine scarf in place on her yellow head
Nor her breasts covered with the light material
The band had given way and there they are, full of milk.
All her clothes slipped down and the salt waves
Moved them gently as they floated about her:
But she was not bothered about her scarf or drifting clothes.
Her whole heart was on you, Theseus,
Her whole mind, her whole consciousness, were fixed immovably.
Poor girl, whom Erycina made wild with continuous sorrow,
Sowing prickly cares in her heart
From the moment when Theseus

egressus curvis e litoribus Piraei
attigit iniusti regis Cortynia templa.
Nam perhibent olim crudeli peste coactam
Androgeoneae poenas exolvere caedis
electos iuvenes simul et decus innuptarum
Cecropiam solitam esse dapem dare Minotauro.
quis angusta malis cum moenia vexarentur,
ipse suum Theseus pro caris corpus Athenis
proicere optavit potius quam talia Cretam
funera Cecropiae nec funera portarentur;
atque ita nave levi nitens ac lenibus auris
magnanimum ad Minoa venit sedesque superbas.
hunc simul ac cupido conspexit lumine virgo
regia, quam suavis expirans castus odores
lectulus in molli complexu matris alebat,
quales Eurotae progignunt flumina myrtos
aurave distinctos educit verna colores,
non prius ex illo flagrantia declinavit
lumina, quam cuncto concepit corpore flammam
funditus atque imis exarsit tota medullis.
heu misere exagitans immiti corde furores
sancte puer, curis hominum qui gaudia misces,
quaeque regis Golgos quaeque Idalium frondosum,
qualibus incensam iactastis mente puellam
fluctibus in flavo saepe hospite suspirantem!
quantos illa tulit languenti corde timores!
quam tum saepe magis fulgore expalluit auri;
cum saevum cupiens contra contendere monstrum
aut mortem appeteret Theseus aut praemia laudis.
non ingrata tamen frustra munuscula divis
promittens tacito succendit vota labello.
nam velut in summo quatientem bracchia Tauro
quercum aut conigeram sudanti cortice pinum
indomitus turbo contorquens flamine robur
eruit (illa procul radicitus exturbata

Setting forth from the curved shores of Piraeus
Reached the Gortynian temple of the unjust king.
The story is that once, forced by a cruel plague
To compensate for the death of Androgeos,
Cecropia used to give as food to the Minotaur
Selected youths and the best of the unmarried girls.
When his narrow walls were troubled with these evils,
Theseus decided to offer his own body for Athens
Rather than that such living funerals should be carried to Crete.
So, pressing on with light ship and suitable breeze,
He came to the hero Minos and his superb residence.
When the princess saw him, which she did with eagerness,
A scented single bed kept her safe as in her mother's arms,
As the rivers of Eurotas mother the myrtles
Or the spring breeze brings out the different colors:
She did not lower her burning eyes
Till she had caught fire all over her body, and deep inside
Her secret marrow grew hot.
You, miserable boy, who stir up frenzy in your hardhearted fashion
And mix the joys of men with trouble;
And you, queen of Golgi and green Idalium,
On what waves you threw the burning mind of that girl
As she sighed repeatedly for the yellow-haired visitor.
What fears she had in her fainting heart!
How often her face was a cold glitter
When Theseus, anxious to measure himself against the violent monster,
Sought either death or the reward of his heroic operation.
Useless though they were the sacrifices she offered were not unpleasing
As she prayed in silence to the gods.
As a hurricane on top of Taurus
Twists to the center an oak or a sweating pine tree
And fells it (and it falls, torn up by the roots,

prona cadit, late casu cuncta abvia frangens),
sic domito saevum prostravit corpore Theseus
nequiquam vanis iactantem cornua ventis.
inde pedem sospes multa cum laude reflexit
errabunda regens tenui vestigia filo,
ne labyrintheis e flexibus egredientem
tecti frustraretur inobservabilis error.

Sed quid ego a primo digressus carmine plura
commemorem, ut linquens genitoris filia vultum,
ut consanguineae complexum, ut denique matris,
quae misera in gnata deperdita leta,
omnibus his Thesei dulcem praeoptarit amorem,
aut ut vecta ratis spumosa ad litora Diae,
venerit aut ut eam devinctam lumina somno
liquerit immemori discedens pectore coniunx?
saepe illam perhibent ardenti corde furentem
clarisonas imo fudisse e pectore voces,
ac tum praeruptos tristem conscendere montes,
unde aciem in pelagi vastos protenderet aestus,
tum tremuli salis adversas procurrere in undas
mollia nudatae tollentem tegmina surae,
atque haec extremis maestam dixisse querellis,
frigidulos udo singultus ore cientem.

"Sicine me patriis avectam, perfide, ab aris,
perfide, deserto liquisti in litore, Theseu?
sicine discedens neglecto numine divum
immemora, devota domum periuria portas?
nullane res potuit crudelis flectere mentis
consilium? tibi nulla fuit clementia praesto,
immite ut nostri vellet miserescere pectus?
at non haec quondam blanda promissa dedisti
voce mihi; non haec miseram sperare iubebas,
sed conubia laeta, sed optatos hymenaeos:
quae cuncta aerii discerpunt irrita venti.
iam iam nulla viro iuranti femina credat,

Far off, breaking everything in its way)
So Theseus threw down the monster, its body inert,
Its horns thrown back useless in the empty wind.
He came back safe from that, having performed his feat,
Relying on the fine thread to guide his footsteps
So that as he came out of the twisting labyrinth
The unobservable confusion of the building did not frustrate him.
But why should I digress from my original song
To mention these particulars: how the daughter fled
From father, sister and finally from her mother
Who cried her eyes out for the wretched girl;
How she preferred the love of Theseus to all her relations;
How the ship sailed for the breakers on the shores of Dia;
Or how her husband left her when she was asleep
Going away without a thought?
It is said that frequently, in her fury, her heart blazing,
She expressed her inmost feelings with resounding screams.
First she would sadly climb up the steep hills
From which she could extend her gaze over the wide sea;
Then she would rush out into the trembling waves,
Lifting her skirt up to her knees
And so, in her final misery, she would say,
Her face wet, her sobs growing cold:
'So, Theseus, you cheat, having taken me from my father's house,
You leave me alone on this remote bit of coast?
So you go away as if there were no gods
And take home nothing but your perjury?
Could nothing have any influence on your cruel mind?
Had you no pity, could you feel nothing at all for me?
You talked blandly enough when you gave me your promises;
You didn't tell me that I was going to be miserable,
You talked about a happy engagement and a desirable marriage:
But all that has been scattered now by the wind.
In future no woman should believe any man's assurances

nulla viri speret sermones esse fideles;
quis dum aliquid cupiens animus praegestit apisci,
nil metuunt iurare, nihil promittere parcunt:
sed simul ac cupidae mentis satiata libidost,
dicta nihil metuere, nihil periuria curant.
certe ego te in medio versantem turbine leti
eripui, et potius germanum amittere crevi,
quam tibi fallaci supremo in tempore dessem;
pro quo dilaceranda feris dabor alitibusque
praeda, neque iniacta tumulabor mortua terra.
quaenam te genuit sola sub rupe leaena?
quod mare conceptum spumantibus expuit undis,
quae Syrtis, quae Scylla rapax, quae vasta Charybdis,
talia qui reddis pro dulci praemia vita?
si tibi non cordi fuerant conubia nostra,
saeva quod horrebas prisci praecepta parentis,
at tamen in vostras potuisti ducere sedes,
quae tibi iucundo famularer serva labore,
candida permulcens liquidis vestigia lymphis
purpureave tuum consternens veste cubile.

Sed quid ego ignaris nequiquam conquerar auris,
externata malo, quae nullis sensibus auctae
nec missas audire queunt nec reddere voces?
ille autem prope iam mediis versatur in undis,
nec quisquam apparet vacua mortalis in alga.
sic nimis insultans extremo tempore saeva
fors etiam nostris invidit questibus auris.

Iuppiter omnipotens, utinam ne tempore primo
Gnosia Cecropiae tetigissent litora puppes,
indomito nec dira ferens stipendia tauro
perfidus in Creta religasset navita funem,
nec malus hic celans dulci crudelia forma
consilia in nostris requiesset sedibus hospes!
nam quo me referam? quali spe perdita nitor?
Idoneosne petam montes? a, gurgite lato
discernens ponti truculentum ubi dividit aequor?

Or hope that anything a man says will come true.
When they want something and are keen to get it
Men will swear anything, and promise anything you like.
But as soon as desire is satisfied
It doesn't matter what they've said, they don't mind perjury.
Yet I saved you when you were caught in the whirlwind of death
And made up my mind to let my brother go
Rather than fail you, but you let me down.
For this I am left to wild beasts and birds of prey
Without decent burial.
Were you born of a lioness under a desert rock?
What sea brought you forth out of the foaming waves,
What Syrtis, rapacious Scylla, monstrous Charybdis,
That you should make such return for saving your life?
If you could not find it in your heart to marry me
Because you were afraid of your peevish father
You could still have taken me home with you
So that I could be your slave, I shouldn't mind the work,
Pouring water gently over your white feet
Or setting the purple cover on your bed.
'But why should I complain to the ignorant winds?
It is useless; I am mad; and the air has no sense—
It can neither hear what I say nor return an answer.
He is already away on the high seas
And there is no soul among all this seaweed.
Even fortune in this extreme hour
Refuses to listen to what I have to say.
'Almighty Jupiter, I wish the Cecropian ship
Had never got so far as the Gnosian coast
Bringing the wild bull its terrible tribute
Or that the cheat had never tied up his boat in Crete
Nor, hiding his cruel designs in a fair appearance
Had ever been a visitor in our house.
Where shall I go from here? What hope shall I entertain?
Shall I take refuge in the hills of Sidon?
The sea is broad and fierce that divides me from them.

an patris auxilium sperem? quemne ipsa reliqui,
respersum iuvenem fraterna caede secuta?
coniugis an fido consoler memet amore,
quine fugit lentos incurvans gurgite remos?
praeterea nullo litus, sola insula, tecto,
nec patet egressus pelagi cingentibus undis:
nulla fugae ratio, nulla spes: omnia muta,
omnia sunt deserta, ostentant omnia letum.
non tamen ante mihi languescent lumina morte,
nec prius a fesso secedent corpore sensus,
quam iustam a divis exposcam prodita multam,
caelestumque fidem postrema comprecer hora.

Quare facta virum multantes vindice poena,
Eumenides, quibus anguino redimita capillo
frons expirantis praeportat pectoris iras,
huc huc adventate, meas audite querellas,
quas ego, vae, misera extremis proferre medullis
cogor inops, ardens, amenti caeca furore.
quae quoniam verae nascuntur pectore ab imo,
vos nolite pati nostrum vanescere luctum;
sed quali solam Theseus me mente reliquit,
tali mente, deae, funestet seque suosque."

Has postquam maestro profudit pectore voces,
supplicium saevis exposcens anxia factis,
annuit invicto caelestum numine rector,
quo motu tellus atque horrida contremuerunt
aequora concussitque micantia sidera mundus.
ipse autem caeca mentem caligine Theseus
consitus oblito dimisit pectore cuncta,
quae mandata prius constanti mente tenebat,
dulcia nec maestro sustollens signa parenti
sospitem Erechtheum se ostendit visere portum.

Namque ferunt olim, classi cum moenia divae
linquentem gnatum ventis concrederet Aegeus,
talia complexum iuveni mandata dedisse.

Shall I look for my father's help? I abandoned him
To follow the young man who killed my brother.
Shall I console myself with the faithful love of my husband?
He is leaving me, bending to dip his oars in the sea.
Here I am on the shores of a desert island;
I am surrounded by sea and there is no way out.
There is no possibility of escape; no hope; all is silence;
All is deserted and everything looks like death.
But I will not allow my eyes to sink into darkness
Nor my tired body to become insensible
Before I have demanded vengeance from the gods
And prayed for the faith of heaven in my last hour.
'Eumenides, avengers of what men do,
Your foreheads decorated with snaky hair
Make public the anger steaming from your hearts:
Come this way now, listen to my complaints
Which I, poor girl, extract from my inmost marrow.
I am driven, I cannot help it, blazing and blind
With mindless fury. Since these griefs come from my heart
Do not let them vanish;
But as Theseus had a mind to leave me
May that mind, goddesses, destroy him and all who are with him.'
When she had poured out these words from her mourning heart,
Demanding that the man who had hurt her should be made to suffer,
The ruler of heaven nodded his powerful assent.
At that the sea and land trembled together;
Earth shook the glittering stars.
Theseus himself, lost in a blank perplexity,
His mind forgetful, failed to keep any hold
Of the instructions he had carried carefully for so long.
He gave no signal to his mourning father
To show that he was safe in sight of the Erechthean harbor.
It is said that when Aegeus entrusted his son to the winds
And the young man left the goddess's town
He embraced him and gave him these instructions:

"Gnate mihi longa iucundior unice vita,
reddite in extrema nuper mihi fine senectae,
gnate, ego quem in dubios cogor dimittere casus,
quandoquidem fortuna mea ac tua fervida virtus
eripit invito mihi te, cui languida, nondum
lumina sunt gnati cara saturata figura:
non ego te gaudens laetanti pectore mittam,
nec te ferre sinam fortunae signa secundae,
sed primum multas expromam mente querellas,
canitiem terra atque infuso pulvere foedans;
inde infecta vago suspendam lintea malo,
nostros ut luctus nostraeque incendia mentis
carbasus obscurata dicet ferrugine Hibera.
quod tibi si sancti concesserit incola Itoni,
quae nostrum genus ac sedes defendere Erechthei
annuit, ut tauri respergas sanguine dextram,
tum vero facito ut memori tibi condita corde
haec vigeant mandata, nec ulla oblitteret aetas,
ut simul ac nostros invisent lumina collis,
funestam antennae deponant undique vestem,
candidaque intorti sustollant vela rudentes,
quam primum cernens ut laeta gaudia mente
agnoscam, cum te reducem aetas prospera sistet."

Haec mandata prius constanti mente tenentem
Thesea ceu pulsae ventorum flamine nubes
aerium nivei montis liquere cacumen.
at pater, ut summa prospectum ex arce petebat,
anxia in assiduos absumens lumina fletus,
cum primum inflati conspexit lintea veli,
praecipitem sese scopulorum e vertice iecit,
amissum credens immiti Thesea fato
sic funesta domus ingressus tecta paterna
morte ferrox Theseus qualem Minoidi luctum
obtulerat mente immemori talem ipse recepit.
quae tum prospectans cedentem maesta carinam
multiplices animo volvebat saucia curas.

'My only son, dearer to me than long life,
Given back to me at the end of old age,
Son, whom I was forced to send on a difficult mission,
Since my fortune and your courage
Took you away from me in spite of my unwillingness
And although my eyes could not see enough of you before they failed:
I will not let you go cheerfully
Nor allow you to bear the marks of a favorable fortune
But first I will express from my mind many complaints,
My gray hair covered with earth and ash to dirty it;
Then I will hang dyed sails on your swaying mast
So that the canvas may show, by its steely blue
My grief and the fire in my heart.
But if she who inhabits the sacred Itonus,
Willing to defend our race and the land of Erechtheus,
Allows you to spray your right hand with the blood of the bull
Be sure that these instructions sprout in your heart
And that no passage of time kills them:
As soon as you set eyes on our hills
Haul down the funereal canvas from your mast
And let the twisted cords run up white sails
So that at the first glance I can see the news is good
When in a happy time you are carried home.'
At first Theseus kept these instructions steadily in mind:
Then, like clouds moved by the breath of winds
From a snowy peak, they left him.
But the father, as he looked out from his rock on the Acropolis
Consuming his eyes with tears, for he wept continually,
As soon as he saw the canvas of the inflated sail
Threw himself headlong from the top of the rock
Believing Theseus lost by ungentle fate.
So ferocious Theseus, entering his father's house,
Found it in mourning, and himself received
Such grief as by forgetting he had given Minos's daughter.
She meanwhile, mournfully watching the ship recede
Stricken, felt her many cares turn in her head.

At parte ex alia florens volitabat Iacchus
cum thiaso Satyrorum et Nysigenis Silenis,
te quaerens, Ariadna, tuoque incensus amore.

* * *

qui tum alacres passim lymphata mente furebant
euhoe bacchantes, euhoe capita inflectentes.
Harum pars tecta quatiebant cuspide thyrsos.
pars e divulso iactabant membra iuvenco.
pars sese tortis serpentibus incingebant,
pars obscura cavis celebrabant orgia cistis,
orgia, quae frustra cupiunt audire profani;
plangebant aliae proceris tympana palmis
aut tereti tenues tinnitus aere ciebant.
multis raucisonos efflabant cornua bombos,
barbaraque horribili stridebat tibia cantu.
Talibus amplifice vestis decorata figuris
pulvinar complexa suo velabat amictu.
quae postquam cupide spectando Thessala pubes
expletast, sanctis coepit decedere divis.
hic, qualis flatu placidum mare matutino
horrificans Zephyrus proclivis incitat undas
Aurora exoriente vagi sub limina Solis,
quae tarde primum clementi flamine pulsae
procedunt, leviterque sonant plangore cachinni,
post vento crescente magis magis increbrescunt
purpureaque procul nantes ab luce refulgent,
sic ibi vestibuli linquentes regia tecta
ad se quisque vago passim pede discedebant.
Quorum post abitum princeps e vertice Peli
advenit Chiron portans silvestria dona;
nam quoscumque ferunt campi, quos Thessala magnis
montibus ora creat, quos propter fluminis undas
aura aperit flores tepidi fecunda Favoni,
hos indistinctis plexos tulit ipse corollis,
quo permulsa domus iucundo risit odore.

In another part the flowering Iacchus was wandering
With a dance of Satyrs and Sileni from Nysa
Looking for you, Ariadne, and burning with love.

* * *

Who then, now here, now there, out of their minds, frenzied,
Shouted Euhoe we are drunk, Euhoe, and their heads swayed.
Some of the women shook long rods with covered points,
Some of them threw in the air the parts of a bull,
Some pulled round themselves a belt of twisted snakes,
Some thronged around the box which held the orgies,
The orgies which only initiates may be told of;
Others struck timbrels with their palms uplifted
Or made slight tinklings with the polished brass:
Many blew horns and made a raucous noise
And barbarian pipes screamed out their horrible tunes.
A covering decorated with figures like these
Hung round the bed and wrapped it up in its folds;
The youth of Thessaly had to have a good look:
When they had done, they began to make way for the gods.
Then as, scaring the sea with his morning breath,
Zephyrus wrinkles the surface of the water
When Dawn rises on the threshold of the journeying sun;
The waves come softly at first, driven by a light wind;
They sound lightly and their complaint is like laughter
But, the wind rising, they grow bigger and bigger
And shine brilliantly as they swim far from the crimson light:
So here, leaving the gates of the royal palace,
The guests depart, each his own way, and scatter.
When they had gone away, from the top of Pelion
Came Chiron with sylvan gifts:
Flowers of the field, flowers from the towering mountains
Of Thessaly, flowers which, by flowering rivers,
The warm, productive breath of Favonius opens:
All these he brings woven together in garlands;
Their pleasant, soothing odor makes the house smile.

confestim Penios adest, viridantia Tempe,
Tempe, quae silvae cingunt super impendentes,
Doris celebranda choreis,
non vacuus: namque ille tulit radicitus altas
fagos ac recto proceras stipite laurus,
non sine nutanti platano lentaque sorore
flammati Phaethontis et aeria cupressu.
haec circum sedes late contexta locavit,
vestibulum ut molli velatum fronde vireret.
post hunc consequitur sollerti corde Prometheus,
extenuata gerens veteris vestigia poenae,
quam quondam silici restrictus membra catena
persolvit pendens e verticibus praeruptis.
inde pater divum sancta cum coniuge natisque
advenit, caelo te solum, Phoebe, relinquens
unigenamque simul cultricem monitibus Idri:
Pelea nam tecum pariter soror aspernatast
nec Thetidis taedas voluit celebrare iugalis.

Qui postquam niveis flexerunt sedibus artus,
large multiplici constructae sunt dape mensae,
cum interea infirmo quatientes corpora motu
veridicos Parcae coeperunt edere cantus.
his corpus tremulum complectens undique vestis
candida purpurea talos incinxerat ora,
at roseae niveo residebant vertice vittae,
aeternumque manus carpebant rite laborem.
laeva colum molli lana retinebat amictum,
dextera tum leviter deducens fila supinis
formabat digitis, tum prono in pollice torquens
libratum tereti versabat turbine fusum,
atque ita decerpens aequabat semper opus dens,
laneaque aridulis haerebant morsa labellis,
quae prius in levi fuerant extantia filo:
ante pedes autem candentis mollia lanae
vellera virgati custodibant calathisci.

Suddenly Peneus is there: he has left Tempe,
Green Tempe, surrounded by hanging forests,
And thronged with Doric dancers:
Not empty-handed, for he was carrying immense beeches
Torn up by the roots, and bay trees with upright stems,
Luxuriant plane trees and tall cypresses
And swaying poplars, sisters of the sun.
With all these he decorated the house
So that the doorway was covered with gentle foliage.
After him came Prometheus, who had thought deeply
And was still marked by the penalty he had paid
When chained to the rocks he was left hanging from a peak.
Then came the father of the gods, the goddess his wife, and his sons,
Leaving you alone in the sky, Phoebus,
With your sister who also lives on the mountains of Idrus,
Like you, your sister regarded Peleus with contempt
And declined to celebrate the marriage of Thetis.
When they had relaxed on the white couches
At tables piled with a varied wedding breakfast,
Then, shaking their bodies weakly,
The Parcae began to emit their reliable chants.
The white gown enfolding their trembling bodies
Came down to the ankles with a purple border;
Their white hair had roses in it;
Their hands, duly engaged in their eternal labor,
The left hand held the distaff covered in wool;
The right hand pulled down the threads while the fingers molded them.
Then the thumb twirled the spindle with a smooth twirl
And all the while they bit off the straggling ends
And the ends they bit off stuck to their dried-up lips
As before they had stuck out from the smooth yarn.
At their feet fleeces of shining wool
Were stored in wicker baskets.

haec tum clarisona pellentes vellera voce
talia divino fuderunt carmine fata,
carmine, perfidiae quod post nulla arguet aetas.

O decus eximium magnis virtutibus augens,
Emathiae tutamen opis, clarissime nato,
accipe, quod laeta tibi pandunt luce sorores,
veridicum oraclum. sed vos, quae fata sequuntur,
   currite ducentes subtegmina, currite, fusi.

adveniet tibi iam portans optata maritis
Hesperus, adveniet fausto cum sidere coniunx,
quae tibi flexanimo mentem perfundat amore
languidulosque paret tecum coniungere somnos,
levia substernens robusto bracchia collo.
   currite ducentes subtegmina, currite, fusi.

nulla domus tales umquam contexit amores,
nullus amor tali coniunxit foedere amantes,
qualis adest Thetidi, qualis concordia Peleo.
   currite ducentes subtegmina, currite, fusi.

nascetur vobis expers terroris Achilles,
hostibus haud tergo, sed forti pectore notus,
qui persaepe vago victor certamine cursus
flammea praevertet celeris vestigia cervae.
   currite ducentes subtegmina, currite, fusi.

non illi quisquam bello se conferet heros,
cum Phrygii Teucro manabunt sanguine rivi,
Troicaque obsidens longinquo moenia bello
periuri Pelopis vastabit tertius heres.
   currite ducentes subtegmina, currite, fusi.

The Parcae struck them and poured out with unmistakable voice
These prophecies in their divine song.
A song the truth of which no time will question:

'To your distinguished name you add great deeds,
Guardian of Thessaly, friend to the child of Ops:
Accept what this happy day the sisters open to you,
The true oracle. And the fates that follow:
Spindles run on, and draw the future out.

'Soon he will come who brings the married what they want,
Hesperus; your wife will come with that happy star.
Like dew upon your mind she will bend it down
And then she will join you in the softest sleep
With her smooth arms under your robust neck.
Spindles run on, and draw the future out.

'No house has ever covered loves like these:
No love has ever joined two with such trust
As is between Peleus and Thetis now.
Spindles run on, and draw the future out.

'Achilles shall be born, and know no fear;
His enemies will never see his back.
How often will he run long distances,
His feet like flames, and faster than a stag.
Spindles run on, and draw the future out.

'No hero shall withstand this man in war
When all the streams of Phrygia flow with blood
And the third heir of perjured Pelops comes
After long war to break the walls of Troy.
Spindles run on, and draw the future out.

illius egregias virtutes claraque facta
saepe fatebuntur gnatorum in funere matres.
cum incultum cano solvent a vertice crinem
putridaque infirmis variabunt pectora palmis.
  currite ducentes subtegmina, currite, fusi.

namque velut densas praecerpens cultor aristas
sole sub ardenti flaventia demetit arva,
Troiugenum infesto prosternet corpora ferro.
  currite ducentes subtegmina, currite, fusi.

testis erit magnis virtutibus unda Scamandri,
quae passim rapido diffunditur Hellesponto,
cuius iter caesis angustans corporum acervis
alta tepefaciet permixta flumina caede.
  currite ducentes subtegmina, currite, fusi.

denique testis erit morti quoque reddita praeda,
cum teres excelso coacervatum aggere bustum
excipiet niveos percussae virginis artus.
  currite ducentes subtegmina, currite, fusi.

nam simul ac fessis dederit fors copiam Archivis
urbis Dardaniae Neptunia solvere vincla,
alta Polyxenia madefient caede sepulcra,
quae, velut ancipiti succumbens victima ferro,
proiciet truncum submisso poplite corpus.
  currite ducentes subtegmina, currite, fusi.

quare agite optatos animi coniungite amores.
accipiat coniunx felici foedere divam,
dedatur cupido iamdudum nupta marito.
  currite ducentes subtegmina, currite, fusi.

'His virtues and remarkable performances
Mothers will know of when their sons are buried;
They will let down their hair from their white heads
And bruise their withered breasts with their weak hands.
  Spindles run on, and draw the future out.

'For as the farmer chops the ears of corn,
Harvesting yellow fields in the hot sun,
His hostile sword will cut the Trojans down.
  Spindles run on, and draw the future out.

'Scamander's waters shall be witnesses
Where they pour out upon the Hellespont,
For he is going to block their way with corpses
And warm the deepest of them with his slaughter.
  Spindles run on, and draw the future out.

'The last witness shall be his prey in death
When the round barrow in its heaped up mound
Receives the white limbs of a girl struck down.
  Spindles run on, and draw the future out.

'For when fortune gives the weary Argives strength
To break the chains about the Dardanian town
They will wet the great tomb with Polyxena's blood.
She, like a victim falling to a sword
Will let her body go and bend her knee.
  Spindles run on, and draw the future out.

'Come therefore, join the loves you so desire.
Husband, now take the goddess in all trust:
Bride, give yourself now to your impatient husband.
  Spindles run on, and draw the future out.

non illam nutrix orienti luce revisens
hesterno collum poterit circumdare filo,
anxia nec mater discordis maesta puellae
secubitu caros mittet sperare nepotes.
currite ducentes subtegmina, currite, fusi.

Talia praefantes quondam felicia Pelei
carmina divino cecinerunt pectore Parcae.
praesentes namque ante domos invisere castas
heroum et sese mortali ostendere coetu
caelicolae nondum spreta pietate solebant.
saepe pater divum templo in fulgente revisens
annua cum festis venissent sacra diebus,
conspexit terra centum procumbere tauros.
saepe vagus Liber Parnasi vertice summo
Thyadas effusis euantis crinibus egit,
cum Delphi tota certatim ex urbe ruentes
acciperent laeti divum fumantibus aris.
saepe in letifero belli certamine Mavors
aut rapidi Tritonis era aut Rhamnusia virgo
armatas hominumst praesens hortata catervas.
sed postquam tellus scelerest imbuta nefando,
iustitiamque omnes cupida de mente fugarunt,
perfudere manus fraterno sanguine fratres,
destitit extinctos natus lugere parentes,
optavit genitor primaevi funera nati,
liber ut innuptae poteretur flore novercae,
ignaro mater substernens se impia nato
impia non veritast divos scelerare parentes:
omnia fanda nefanda malo permixta furore
iustificam nobis mentem avertere deorum.
quare nec tales dignantur visere coetus,
nec se contingi patiuntur lumine claro.

'When the nurse comes to see her in the morning
She will find that yesterday's thread won't go round her neck
Nor will her worrying mother have to fear,
Because the girl has slept alone, she will have no grandchildren.
Spindles run on, and draw the future out.'

Such happiness was pronounced for Peleus
And so the Parcae sang from divine hearts.
For in those days the Fates appeared in person,
Visited chaste homes and showed themselves to mortals
But that was before religion was despised.
The father of the gods, visiting his bright temple
When the annual rites came round on his festal days,
Would watch a hundred bulls felled to the ground.
Often Liber, wandering on the top of Parnassus,
Drove before him the Thyades with streaming hair,
When all the Delphians racing out of their city
Received him gladly and with smoking altars.
Often in the middle of a murderous battle Mavors,
The mistress of swift Triton or the Rhamnusian Virgin
Appeared in the armed bands to encourage them.
But when the whole world was imbued with crime
And so put justice out of its greedy mind
Brothers dipped their hands in their brothers' blood,
The son no longer mourned his father's death,
The father wished for the death of his vigorous son
So that he could enjoy the flower of the bride,
The mother, getting secretly underneath her son,
Did not scruple to sin against the ancestral gods,
Then right and wrong were confused in an evil frenzy
And that turned from us the just minds of the gods.
So they no longer deign to come among us
Nor can they bear to be touched by the clear light.

LXV

Etsi me assiduo confectum cura dolore
  sevocat a doctis, Hortale, virginibus,
nec potis est dulcis Musarum expromere fetus
  mens animi, tantis fluctuat ipsa malis:
namque mei nuper Lethaeo gurgite fratris
  pallidulum manans alluit unda pedem,
Troia Rhoeteo quem subter litore tellus
  ereptum nostris obterit ex oculis.

* * *

alloquar, audiero numquam tua facta loquentem,
  numquam ego te, vita frater amabilior,
aspiciam posthac. at certe semper amabo,
  semper maesta tua carmina morte canam,
qualia sub densis ramorum concinit umbris
  Daulias absumpti fata gemens Ityli.
sed tamen in tantis maeroribus, Hortale, mitto
  haec expressa tibi carmina Battiadae,
ne tua dicta vagis nequiquam credita ventis
  effluxisse meo forte putes animo,
ut missum sponsi furtivo munere malum
  procurrit casto virginis e gremio,
quod miserae oblitae molli sub veste locatum,
  dum adventu matris prosilit, excutitur:
atque illud prono praeceps agitur decursu,
  huic manat tristi conscius ore rubor.

LXV

Although I am exhausted by continual grief
And sorrow calls me away from the Muses, Hortalus;
Nor can what is in my mind be expressed in verse
So great is the trouble that shakes me:
For my brother has descended to Lethe,
The water is lapping his pale foot;
Under the coast of Rhoeteum the earth of Troy
Lies heavily on him, and he has gone from our sight.

* * *

I shall never again speak to you or hear you speaking
Nor shall I ever, brother dearer than life,
See you again. But certainly I shall love you,
I shall always have you in mind in my poems
As among the branches and in heavy shadows
Daulias cries over the fate of Itylus.
Yet in the middle of this mourning, Hortalus, I send you
These translations from Battiades,
So that you will not think I have forgotten what you said
Nor that it was as if you had spoken to the wind.
It is as if an apple sent to a girl by her lover
Fell out of her decorously covered bosom
When she, having put it in a fold of her gown and then forgotten it,
Is startled by the approach of her mother:
Then see how quickly it rolls down and away
And a self-conscious redness creeps over her regretful face.

LXVI

Omnia qui magni dispexit lumina mundi,
  qui stellarum ortus comperit atque obitus,
flammeus ut rapidi solis nitor obscuretur,
  ut cedant certis sidera temporibus,
ut Triviam furtim sub Latmia saxa relegans
  dulcis amor gyro devocet aerio,
idem me ille Conon caelesti in lumine vidit
  e Beroniceo vertice caesariem
fulgentem clare, quam multis illa dearum
  levia protendens bracchia pollicitast,
qua rex tempestate novo auctus hymenaeo
  vastatum finis iverat Assyrios,
dulcia nocturnae portans vestigia rixae,
  quam de virgineis gesserat exuviis.
estne novis nuptis odio Venus atque parentum
  frustrantur falsis gaudia lacrimulis,
ubertim thalami quas intra limina fundunt?
  non, ita me divi, vera gemunt, iuerint.
id mea me multis docuit regina querellis
  invisente novo proelia torva viro.
at tu non orbum luxti deserta cubile,
  sed fratris cari flebile discidium!
quam penitus maestas exedit cura medullas!
  ut tibi tum toto pectore sollicitae
sensibus ereptis mens excidit! at te ego certe
  cognoram a parva virgine magnanimam.
anne bonum oblita's facinus, quo regium adepta's
  coniugium, quod non fortior ausit alis?
sed tum maesta virum mittens quae verba locuta's!
  Iuppiter, ut tristi lumina saepe manu!
quis te mutavit tantus deus? an quod amantes
  non longe a caro corpore abesse volunt?
atque ibi me cunctis pro dulci coniuge divis
  non sine taurino sanguine pollicita's,
si reditum tetulisset. is haud in tempore longo

LXVI

He identified all the stars in the sky,
Finding out when they rose and when they set,
How the brilliant flame of the sun is eclipsed,
How the stars withdraw at determined times,
How Trivia is to be found in a cave on Latmus
When sweet love calls her down from her aery circuit.
This was Conon: then he saw me in the stars,
I who am the hair from Berenice's head,
Shining brightly. She vowed me to many goddesses
Stretching her gentle arms up as she did so
At the time when the king, in the honor of his new marriage
Had gone to devastate the Assyrian frontiers,
Still disheveled from the nocturnal struggles
He had lately waged to strip and despoil a virgin.
Do brides indeed hate Venus, and when their parents
Show joy, do you suppose it is genuine blubbering
They make as they enter the door of the marriage chamber?
No, help me gods, their moaning is all dissembled.
My queen at least taught me that with her lamentation
When her newly married husband went off to the war.
But you of course weren't bewailing an empty bed;
The loss of a brother gave you something to cry about!
And how profoundly that sorrow ate at your heart!
You were so anxious the whole of you seemed involved;
Your senses left you, your mind gave way. Yet I for certain
Knew you had courage enough as a little girl.
Have you forgotten the magnificent crime you committed
Which no one else would have dared, for a royal marriage?
But in sending out your husband what words were spoken!
Jupiter, how your sad hand rubbed at your eyes!
Some great god must have changed you! Or may be lovers
Don't like their favorite body too long away?
So I with the blood of bulls had to be sacrificed
For your dear husband, to all the gods if he came back.
That was the vow. It didn't take him very long

captam Asiam Aegypti finibus addiderat.
quis ego pro factis caelesti reddita coetu
pristina vota novo munere dissoluo.
invita, o regina, tuo de vertice cessi,
invita: adiuro teque tuumque caput,
digna ferat quod siquis inaniter adiurarit:
sed qui se ferro postulet esse parem?
ille quoque eversus mons est, quem maximum in oris
progenies Thiae clara supervehitur,
cum Medi peperere novum mare, cumque iuventus
per medium classi barbara navit Athon.
quid facient crines, cum ferro talia cedant?
Iuppiter, ut Chalybon omne genus pereat
et qui principio sub terra quaerere venas
institit ac ferri stringere duritiem!
abiunctae paulo ante comae mea fata sorores
lugebant, cum se Memnonis Aethiopis
unigena impellens nutantibus aera pennis
obtulit Arsinoes Locridos alisequos,
isque per aetherias me tollens avolat umbras
et Veneris casto collocat in gremio.
ipsa suum Zephyritis eo famulum legarat,
Graia Canopeis incola litoribus.
inde Venus vario ne solum in lumine caeli
ex Ariadneis aurea temporibus
fixa corona foret, sed nos quoque fulgeremus
devotae flavi verticis exuviae,
uvidulam a fletu cedentem ad templa deum me
sidus in antiquis diva novum posuit:
Virginis et saevi contingens namque Leonis
lumina, Callisto iuncta Lycaoniae,
vertor in occasum, tardum dux ante Booten,
qui vix sero alto mergitur Oceano.
sed quamquam me nocte premunt vestigia divum,
lux autem canae Tethyi restituit,
(pace tua fari hic liceat, Rhamnusia virgo,

To capture Asia and add it to Egypt's territories.
And so it was done: and I was given up to the divinities
And paid for yesterday's vow with an offering today.
I was not very anxious, queen, to come off the top of you,
Not anxious: I will swear that by you and your head
And if anyone forswears that, let him have his deserts.
But who is there, after all, who can stand up to steel?
Even that mountain was turned upside down, the biggest there was
In all the shores the son of Thia drives over,
When the Medes produced a new sea, and the youthful barbarians
Took their fleet right through the middle of Athos.
What can you expect of hair, when steel makes things like that shudder?
O Jupiter, let the whole race of the Chalybes perish
With the man who began it by looking for veins underground
And first invented the way of making pig iron!
The sister hairs were just bewailing the fate
Of me that was taken from them, when Ethiop Memnon's
Brother appeared, and flapping about with his wings,
Carried me off—he is Arsinoe's flying horse.
He bears me aloft through the ethereal shadows
And dumps me down in the chaste bosom of Venus.
Zephyritis herself had despatched her man on the mission,
The Grecian lady who lives on the shores of Canopus.
So Venus, who thought that the light of heaven should have something
Besides the golden coronet of Ariadne
And that it would be a good thing if we also shone there,
We the sacrificed spoil of your yellow head.
Put me all wet with weeping in the temples of the gods
As a new constellation among the old ones: she was a goddess.
You will find me among the stars next to Virgo and Leo,
Quite near to Callisto who was the daughter of Lycaon.
I turn to the west, and get there before the Bootes
Who even at a late hour will hardly dip in the sea.
However, at night, the steps of the gods press upon me,
I am back with the white-headed Tethys when the day comes.
(I hope you'll allow me to say this, Virgin of Rhamnus,

namque ego non uilo vera timore tegam.
nec si me infestis discerpent sidera dictis,
condita quin veri pectoris evoluam):
non his tam laetor rebus, quam me afore semper,
afore me a dominae vertice discrucior,
quicum ego, dum virgo quondam fuit, omnibus expers
unguentis, una milia multa bibi.
nunc vos, optato cum iunxit lumine taeda,
non prius unanimis corpora coniugibus
tradite nudantes reiecta veste papillas
quam iucunda mihi munera libet onyx,
vester onyx, casto colitis quae iura cubili.
sed quae se impuro dedit adulterio.
illius a, mala dona levis bibat irrita pulvis:
namque ego ab indignis praemia nulla peto.
sed magis, o nuptae, semper concordia vestras
semper amor sedes incolat assiduus.
tu vero, regina, tuens cum sidera divam
placabis festis luminibus Venerem,
unguinis expertem non siveris esse tuam me,
sed potius largis affice muneribus.
sidera cur retinent? iterum coma regia fiam:
proximus Hydrochoi fulgoret Oarion!

LXVII

O dulci iucunda viro, iucunda parenti,
salve, teque bona Iuppiter auctet ope,
ianua, quam Balbo dicunt servisse benigne
olim, cum sedes ipse senex tenuit,
quamque ferunt rursus nato servire maligne,

You will not find me afraid of telling the truth.
And though the stars will tear me apart with their gossip
I feel I must plainly say what is in my heart.)
I am not so happy, with all this, that I don't suffer
Terribly at being away from the head of my mistress
With whom (although, when a virgin, she didn't use it)
I have, I assure you, drunk many thousands of perfumes.
Now you, when the wedding torch has been lit for you,
Before you give your bodies to your enthusiastic husbands
Or even pull back your dress to show your nipples,
Make me a pleasant gift from your onyx jar
You who are devoting yourselves to the rights of a chaste bed.
But of course if anyone gives herself up to adultery
I hope that the dust will swallow her worthless gifts
For I certainly don't want offerings from people who aren't respectable,
Rather, express a hope that they will live in harmony
And that they will be blessed with an assiduous love.
You, queen, when you look at the stars at evening
And are going to propitiate Venus with festal lamps,
Do not leave your old servant empty-handed
But rather seek my favour with outsized gifts.
Why do the stars keep me here? If I were the queen's once again
Orion could blaze as he liked and be next to Aquarius.

LXVII

Catullus

Pleasing enough to the husband, and pleasing to his father,
Hullo, front door, and Jupiter's blessings on you!
They say that you served Balbus kindly enough
When the old man was alive and had this house.
Now they report you're serving the son unkindly

postquam est porrecto facta marita sene.
dic agedum nobis, quare mutata feraris
in dominum veterem deseruisse fidem.

"non (ita Caecilio placeam, cui tradita nunc sum)
cupla meast, quamquam dicitur esse mea,
nec peccatum a me quisquam pote dicere quicquam:
verum istius populi ianua qui te facit,
qui, quacumque aliquid reperitur non bene factum,
ad me omnes clamant: ianua, culpa tuast."

non istuc satis est uno te dicere verbo,
sed facere ut quivis sentiat et videat.

"qui possum? nemo quaerit nec scire laborat."

nos volumus: nobis dicere ne dubita.

"primum igitur, virgo quod fertur tradita nobis,
falsumst. non illam vir prior attigerat,
languidior tenera cui pendens sicula beta
numquam se mediam sustulit ad tunicam:
sed pater illius gnati violasse cubile
dicitur et miseram conscelerasse domum;
sive quod impia mens caeco flagrabat amore,
seu quod iners sterili semine natus erat,
et quaerendum unde unde foret nervosius illud,
quod posset zonam solvere virgineam."

Since the old man is stiff and the bride has come here.
Tell me, how is it you are said to have changed
And abandoned your dutiful conduct towards your master?

Door

No offense to Caecilius, whose property I now am,
But it's not my fault, although they say it is;
No one ever caught me doing anything wrong.
Of course people will say the door does it all;
When anything goes wrong they all shout out,
'There you are, front door, at it again!'

Catullus

It isn't enough just to put it like that:
You have to try and make yourself understood.

Door

What can I do? Nobody seems to want to know.

Catullus

I want to know, so don't mind telling me.

Door

In the first place it's not true that she was a virgin when she came here:
Her husband wasn't the first to touch her.
His dagger hung limper than a stalk of beet
And never had the strength to make his tunic stick out.
But the father is supposed to have been busy in his son's bed
And to have done worse than bring the house into disrepute;
Either because his beastly mind was in a flaming passion
Or because the son, coming from bad stock, was impotent
And it needed someone with a bit more courage
To loosen a virgin's belt and get her clothes off.

egregium narras mira pietate parentem,
  qui ipse sui gnati minxerit in gremium.

"atqui non solum hoc se dicit cognitum habere
  Brixia Chinea supposita speculae,
flavus quam molli percurrit flumine Melo,
  Brixia Veronae mater amata meae;
sed de Postumio et Corneli narrat amore,
  cum quibus illa malum fecit adulterium."

dixerit hic aliquis: "quid? tu istaec, ianua, nosti?
  cui numquam domini limine abesse licet,
nec populum auscultare, sed hic suffixa tigillo
  tantum operire soles aut aperire domum?"

"saepe illam audivi furtiva voce loquentem
  solam cum ancillis haec sua flagitia,
nomine dicentem quos diximus, ut pote quae mi
  speraret nec linguam esse nec auriculam.
praetera addebat quendam, quem dicere nolo
  nomine, ne tollat rubra supercilia.
longus homost, magnas cui lites intulit olim
  falsum mendaci ventre puerperium."

Catullus

That's a fine story of parental devotion,
The old man pissing in his son's lap.

Door

But that is not the only thing Brixia knows
—The town that lies under the old lookout
And through which Meo flows with its yellow water,
Brixia the mother of my beloved Verona;
It also has stories about Postumius and Cornelius
With whom that woman also had her adventures.

Catullus

Someone will say: 'Hey, door, how can you know all this?
After all you never get away from the house;
You can't hear the talk of the town, fixed to that doorjamb
With nothing to do but to open and shut.'

Door

I have often heard that woman whispering to her maids
And telling them all about her goings on,
Naming the people I have spoken of, hoping no doubt
That I shouldn't be able to hear or repeat what she said.
She also mentioned another name which I won't tell you
In case the man should raise his ginger eyebrows.
He is a tall man, and was once involved in a big lawsuit,
Something to do with misrepresenting a birth and a wrong mother.

LXVIII

Quod mihi fortuna casuque oppressus acerbo
conscriptum hoc lacrimis mittis epistolium,
naufragum ut eiectum spumantibus aequoris undis
sublevem et a mortis limine restituam,
quem neque sancta Venus molli requiescere somno
desertum in lecto caelibe perpetitur,
nec veterum dulci scriptorum carmine Musae
oblectant, cum mens anxia pervigilat;
id gratumst mihi, me quoniam tibi dicis amicum,
muneraque et Musarum hinc petis et Veneris:
sed tibi ne mea sint ignota incommoda, Mani,
neu me odisse putes hospitis officium,
accipe, quis merser fortunae fluctibus ipse,
ne amplius a misero dona beata petas.
tempore quo primum vestis mihi tradita purast,
iucundum cum aetas florida ver ageret,
multa satis lusi: non est dea nescia nostri,
quae dulcem curis miscet amaritiem:
sed totum hoc studium luctu fraterna mihi mors
abstulit. o misero frater adempte mihi,
tu mea tu moriens fregisti commoda, frater,
tecum una totast nostra sepulta domus,
omnia tecum una perierunt gaudia nostra,
quae tuus in vita dulcis alebat amor.
cuius ego interitu tota de mente fugavi
haec studia atque omnes delicias animi.
quare, quod scribis "Veronae turpe Catullo
esse, quod hic quisquis de meliore notast
frigida deserto tepefecit membra cubili,"
id, Mani, non est turpe, magis miserumst.
ignosces igitur, si, quae mihi luctus ademit.
haec tibi non tribuo munera, cum nequeo.
nam, quod scriptorum non magnast copia apud me,

LXVIII

That, oppressed by fortune and a bitter event,
You should send me this note written in tears,
That, shipwrecked and ejected by the foaming waves
You look to me to carry you on shore
When divine Venus refuses her sensual sleep
—For you lie alone in an empty bed
And have not the consolation of reading over the old poets
When your anxious mind keeps you awake—
I am glad of it, since you treat me as a friend
And ask me for provisions from Venus and the Muses:
In case you do not know my own troubles, Manlius,
And think I make a poor return for your hospitality,
I had better tell you I myself am under the waves of fortune
So that you do not look for happiness in this direction.
At the time when I first put on an adult toga
And my flowering years were at their agreeable spring
I played well enough: that goddess is not unknown to me
Who mixes a delightful bitterness with our cares:
But with my brother's death all preoccupations of that kind
Have left me. In sorrow, my brother, I accept your loss;
Dying, you have deprived me of my advantages.
With you all our house is buried;
With you all those joys have died
Which your love kept going while you were alive.
Since your death I have put out of my mind
All such concerns and every kind of pleasure.
You write that I ought to be ashamed of myself staying at Verona
When all the young men about town
Are keeping themselves warm in the bed that used to be mine.
That, Manlius, is not a disgrace but a misfortune.
You will pardon me, therefore, if I do not, because I cannot
Give you those gifts which grief has taken away.
For I haven't got many authors with me here.

hoc fit, quod Romae vivimus: illa domus,
illa mihi sedes, illic mea carpitur aetas:
huc una ex multis capsula me sequitur.
quod cum ita sit, nolim statuas nos mente maligna
id facere aut animo non satis ingenuo,
quod tibi non utriusque petenti copia praesto est:
ultro ego deferrem, copia siqua foret

LXVIIIa

Non possum reticere, deae, qua me Allius in re
iuverit aut quantis iuverit officiis:
ne fugiens saeclis obliviscentibus aetas
illius hoc caeca nocte tegat studium:
sed dicam vobis, vos porro dicite multis
milibus et facite haec charta loquatur anus

* * *

notescatque magis mortuus atque magis,
nec tenuem texens sublimis aranea telam
in deserto Alli nomine opus faciat.
nam mihi quam dederit duplex Amathusia curam,
scitis, et in quo me torruerit genere,
cum tantum arderem quantum Trinacria rupes
lymphaque in Oetaeis Malia Thermopylis,
maesta neque assiduo tabescere lumina fletu
cessarent tristique imbre madere genae.
qualis in aerii perlucens vertice montis
rivus muscoso prosilit e lapide,
qui cum de prona praeceps est valle volutus,
per medium densi transit iter populi,
dulce viatori lasso in sudore levamen,
cum gravis exustos aestus hiulcat agros:
hic, velut in nigro iactatis turbine nautis

That is because I live in Rome. That is where my house is,
My home, that is where I pass my life:
All I bring with me here is one box of books.
In these circumstances I hope you will not consider me ill-natured
Or think I am acting ungenerously
If I have not provided you with either of the things you ask for.
I would provide them unasked, if I had any.

LXVIIIA

I cannot remain silent about how Allius helped me,
Goddesses, what it was and how much he helped.
I do not want time, flying in forgetful centuries,
To bury his efforts in darkness.
So I will tell you, and you hereafter can tell it
To many thousands, when my book grows old.

* * *

Let him become more and more widely known after his death;
And let no spider weaving its delicate web
Cover the name of Allius with forgetfulness
For you know with what cares the ambiguous Amathusian
Visited me and how she oppressed me.
I was burning like the Trinacrian rock
And the Malian waters at Oetean Thermopylae,
My eyes were wasted with continual tears
And my cheeks always wet as if I'd been out in the rain.
As from the top of a high mountain
A stream springs brightly out of the mossy rock
And rolls headlong into the valley,
Then crosses a road thronged with people
And freshens the traveler in his weary sweat
When summer cracks the burning fields:
Or as to sailors caught in a dark storm

lenius aspirans aura secunda venit
iam prece Pollucis, iam Castoris implorata,
tale fuit nobis Allius auxilium.
is clausum lato patefecit limite campum,
isque domum nobis isque dedit dominam,
ad quam communes exerceremus amores.
quo mea se molli candida diva pede
intulit et trito fulgentem in limine plantam
innixa arguta constituit solea;
coniugis ut quondam flagrans advenit amore
Protesilaeam Laudamia domum
inceptam frustra, nondum cum sanguine sacro
hostia caelestis pacificasset eros.
nil mihi tam valde placeat, Rhamnusia virgo,
quod temere invitis suscipiatur eris.
quam ieiuna pium desideret ara cruorem,
doctast amisso Laudamia viro,
coniugis ante coacta novi dimittere collum
quam veniens una atque altera rursus hiemps
noctibus in longis avidum saturasset amorem,
posset ut abrupto vivere coniugio,
quod scibant Parcae non longo tempore abesse,
si miles muros isset ad Iliacos:
nam tum Helenae raptu primores Argivorum
coeperat ad sese Troia ciere viros.
Troia (nefas) commune sepulcrum Asiae Europaeque
Troia virum et virtutum omnium acerba cinis,
quaene etiam nostro letum miserabile fratri
attulit. ei misero frater adempte mihi,
ei misero fratri iucundum lumen ademptum,
tecum una totast nostra sepulta domus;
omnia tecum una peirerunt gaudia nostra,
quae tuus in vita dulcis alebat amor.
quem nunc tam longe non inter nota sepulcra
nec prope cognatos compositum cineres,

Comes a gentler wind blowing from the right quarter
—For which they have prayed to Pollux and then to Castor—
That is what Allius's help was to me.
He threw open the gate into a closed field;
He gave me a house and a mistress
With whom we could practice our pleasures in common.
It was to this house that my candid goddess
Came with soft step and placed her shining foot
On the common threshold, pressing it with her thin shoe,
As once, flaming with love for her husband,
Laodamia came to the house of Protesilaus
Which was never complete, because the blood of a victim
Had not yet pacified the masters of heaven.
May nothing please me overmuch, Rhamnusian virgin,
Which is undertaken without the will of those masters.
How the starved altar desires the blood of sacrifice
Laodamia learned when her man was lost,
Forced to let fall her arms from the neck of her bridegroom
Before the coming of one winter and then another
With their long nights should give her enough of love
So that she would live on with her husband gone.
The Parcae knew he would shortly be lost
If he went as a soldier to the Ilian walls.
For it was then that, because of the rape of Helen,
Troy began to excite against herself all the Argive nobles,
Troy the foul common grave of Asia and Europe,
Troy the bitter ash of men and all their actions
Which also brought pitiful death to my brother.
Brother, you were taken from me, I am unhappy;
The kind light was taken from you, you are unhappy.
With you all our house is buried;
With you all those joys have died
Which your love kept going while you were with us.
Now so far, and not among known tombs,
Having found no place near the ashes of the family,

sed Troia obscena, Troia infelice sepultum
  detinet extremo terra aliena solo.
ad quam tum properans fertur simul undique pubes
  Graeca penetralis deseruisse focos,
ne Paris abducta gavisus libera moecha
  otia pacato degeret in thalamo.
quo tibi tum casu, pulcherrima Laudamia,
  ereptumst vita dulcius atque anima
coniugium: tanto te absorbens vertice amoris
  aestus in abruptum detulerat barathrum,
quale ferunt Grai Pheneum prope Cylleneum
  siccare emulsa pingue palude solum,
quod quondam caesis montis fodisse medullis
  audit falsiparens Amphitryoniades,
tempore quo certa Stymphalia monstra sagitta
  perculit imperio deterioris eri,
pluribus ut caeli tereretur ianua divis,
  Hebe nec longa virginitate foret.
sed tuus altus amor barathro fuit altior illo,
  qui tamen indomitam ferre iugum docuit;
nam nec tam carum confecto aetate parenti
  una caput seri nata nepotis alit,
qui, cum divitiis vix tandem inventus avitis
  nomen testatas intulit in tabulas,
impia derisi gentilis gaudia tollens
  suscitat a cano vulturium capiti:
nec tantum niveo gavisast ulla columbo
  compar, quae multo dicitur improbius
oscula mordenti semper decerpere rostro,
  quam quae praecipue multivolast mulier.
sed tu horum magnos vicisti sola furores,
  ut semel es flavo conciliata viro.
aut nihil aut paulo cui tum concedere digna
  lux mea se nostrum contulit in gremium,
quam circumcursans hinc illinc saepe Cupido

Obscene Troy, cursed Troy keeps you buried
In the extreme soil of an alien land.
To this town at that time all the youth of Greece
Were hurrying, deserting the family shrines
So that Paris should not enjoy his whore in a quiet bed.
By that event, beautiful Laodamia,
Your husband dearer than life of mind was taken from you.
The tide of love sucked you down abruptly,
Carrying you away into its caves and channels
As, the Greeks say, near Cyllenian Pheneus
The soil is drained from the rich marshland
Where the so-called son of Amphytrion
Is supposed to have dug away the bones of the mountain
At the time when he struck the Stymphalian monsters
With a sure arrow on the orders of a worse master
That the gateway of heaven might be thronged by more gods
And Hebe might not long remain a virgin.
But your deep love was deeper than that gulf
And taught you although untamed to bear the yoke:
For not so dear to the man who has completed his age
Is the head of the grandchild whom his daughter nurses,
Who has come at last to inherit the ancestral wealth
Provide a name that can go in the will
And put an end to the expectations of relatives
So driving the vulture from the old man's head:
Nor did ever dove so delight its white mate,
Though they are said always to be snatching kisses
With their mordant beaks, and more shamelessly,
Though women are notably inconstant.
But you alone outdid the madness of all these
When you were brought together with your golden husband.
Little or not at all less deserving was my light
When she gave herself into my lap.
Running around hither and thither Cupid

fulgebat crocina candidus in tunica.
quae tamenetsi uno non est contenta Catullo,
rara verecundae furta feremus erae,
ne nimium simus stultorum more molesti.
saepe etiam Iuno, maxima caelicolum,
coniugis in culpa flagrantem concoquit iram,
noscens omnivoli plurima furta Iovis.
atque nec divis homines componier aequumst,

* * *

ingratum tremuli tolle parentis onus.
nec tamen illa mihi dextra deducta paterna
fragrantem Assyrio venit odore domum,
sed furtiva dedit mira munuscula nocte,
ipsius ex ipso dempta viri gremio.
quare illud satis est, si nobis is datur unis,
quem lapide illa, dies, candidiore notat.

Hoc tibi, quod potui, confectum carmine munus
pro multis, Alli, redditur officiis,
ne vestrum scabra tangat rubigine nomen
haec atque illa dies atque alia atque alia.
huc addent divi quam plurima, quae Themis olim
antiquis solitast munera ferre piis:
sitis felices et tu simul et tua vita
et domus illa, in qua lusimus, et domina,
et qui principio nobis terram dedit aufert
a quo sunt primo mi omnia nata bona.
et longe ante omnes mihi quae me carior ipsost,
lux mea, qua viva vivere dulce mihist.

Shone brilliantly in his saffron cloak.
Yet although she is not satisfied with Catullus alone
I will bear with the rare deceits of this modest lady
Lest I become tiresome like stupid men.
Often indeed Juno, the greatest of the goddesses,
Chokes back her flaming anger at her husband's faults,
Knowing the numerous deceits of all-despising Jove.
And I must not compare men to gods

* * *

Bear the unpleasing weight of a tremulous father.
Still I did not take her from her father's hand
Into a house fragrant with Assyrian odors
But she gave me her furtive gifts in the marvelous night,
Stolen from her husband's bed.
Therefore it is enough if she gives me alone
The day she marks with a white pebble.

This gift, the best I could, set out in verse
Is given you, Allius, for your many kindnesses
So that your name shall not be touched by rust
On this day or the next nor yet the next.
To this the gods will add the many gifts
Themis in former times gave to the pious.
I hope that you and your life may be happy,
The house we played in and its mistress too,
And he who first offered me the earth,
From whom came all the good things I have known.
And far before all, she I love more than myself,
My light, for I am happy as long as she is alive.

LXIX

Noli admirari, quare tibi femina nulla,
  Rufe, velit tenerum supposuisse femur,
non si illam rarae labefactes munere vestis
  aut perluciduli deliciis lapidis.
laedit te quaedam mala fabula, qua tibi fertur
  valle sub alarum trux habitare caper.
hunc metuunt omnes. neque mirum: nam mala valde est
  bestia, nec quicum bella puella cubet.
quare aut crudelem nasorum interfice pestem
  aut admirari desine cur fugiunt.

LXX

Nulli se dicit mulier mea nubere malle
  quam mihi, non si se Iuppiter ipse petat.
dicit: sed mulier cupido quod dicit amanti
  in vento et rapida scribere oportet aqua.

LXXI

Siquoi iure bono sacer alarum obstitit hircus,
  aut siquem merito tarda podagra secat,
aemulus iste, toro qui vestro exercet amorem,
  mirificest a te nactus utrumque malum.
nam quotiens futuit, totiens ulciscitur ambos:
  illam affligit odore, ipse perit podagra.

LXIX

It should not surprise you, Rufus, that no woman
Wants to put her gentle thigh under yours,
That you cannot bribe them with presents of clothes
And that even the most dazzling jewelry is no temptation.
Your trouble is an unfortunate rumor, which reports
That there is a powerful goat under your armpits.
They're all afraid of him. No wonder, he is nasty, without a doubt,
That beast, and not one a beautiful girl would go to bed with.
So, either you should slaughter this cruel offense to their noses
Or cease to express surprise when they run away.

LXX

My woman says there is no one she would rather marry
Than me, not even if Jupiter were to propose to her.
She says: but what a woman says to an eager lover
Ought to be recorded in wind and water.

LXXI

If ever a damned goat got in a man's way
Or anyone was ever tortured and impeded by gout
It is the rival who practices love in your bed.
It is marvelous how this chap has got both of them.
Whenever he has a fuck, they are both in agony.
She is knocked back by the smell and he nearly dies of the gout.

LXXII

Dicebas quondam solum te nosse Catullum,
  Lesbia, nec prae me velle tenere Iovem.
dilexi tum te non tantum ut vulgus amicam,
  sed pater ut gnatos diligit et generos.
nunc te cognovi: quare etsi impensius uror,
  multo mi tamen es vilior et levior.
qui potis est? inquis. quod amantem iniuria talis
  cogit amare magis, sed bene velle minus.

LXXIII

Desine de quoquam quicquam bene velle mereri
  aut aliquem fieri posse putare pium.
omnia sunt ingrata, nihil fecisse benigne;
  immo etiam taedet, taedet obestque magis:
ut mihi, quem nemo gravius nec acerbius urget,
  quam modo qui me unum atque unicum amicum habuit.

LXXIV

Gellius audierat, patruum obiurgare solere
  siquis delicias diceret aut faceret.
hoc ne ipsi accideret, patrui perdepsuit ipsam
  uxorem et patruum reddidit Harpocratem.
quod voluit fecit: nam, quamvis irrumet ipsum
  nunc patruum, verbum non faciet patruus.

LXXII

You used to say that you knew only Catullus,
Lesbia, and that you thought nothing of Jove as compared to me.
I regarded you then not simply as an ordinary girl-friend
But as a father regards his sons and sons-in-law.
Now I have got to know you: and although I burn more than ever
I regard you as a much less valuable person.
How can that be? you ask. Such injuries to a lover
Force him to love more, but to be less benevolent.

LXXIII

Give up wishing to do anyone a kindness
Or thinking that anyone could ever return thanks.
All is without return: to have acted kindly is nothing.
So with me, whom no one oppresses harder or more bitterly
Than the man who until just now called me his one and only friend.

LXXIV

Gellius had heard his uncle was very censorious
If anyone mentioned pleasure or indulged in it.
To keep out of trouble he fucked auntie,
Which worked wonders in keeping uncle quiet.
He did what he liked: for even if he had a go at uncle himself
He could count on uncle never saying a word.

LXXV

Huc est mens deducta tua, mea Lesbia, culpa,
atque ita se officio perdidit ipsa suo,
ut iam nec bene velle queat tibi, si optima fias.
nec desistere amare, omnia si facias.

LXXVI

Siqua recordanti benefacta priora voluptas
est homini, cum se cogitat esse pium,
nec sanctam violasse fidem, nec foedere in ullo
divum ad fallendos numine abusum homines,
multa parata manent in longa aetate, Catulle,
ex hoc ingrato gaudia amore tibi.
nam quaecumque homines bene cuiquam aut dicere possunt
aut facere, haec a te dictaque factaque sunt;
omnia quae ingratae perierunt credita menti.
quare cur tu te iam amplius excrucies?
quin tu animum offirmas atque istinc teque reducis
et dis invitis desinis esse miser?
difficilest longum subito deponere amorem.
difficilest, verum hoc qualubet efficias.
una salus haec est, hoc est tibi pervincendum:
hoc facias, sive id non pote sive pote.
o di, si vestrumst misereri, aut si quibus umquam
extremam iam ipsa in morte tulistis opem,
me miserum aspicite et, si vitam puriter egi,
eripite hanc pestem perniciemque mihi.
heu, mihi surrepens imos ut torpor in artus
expulit ex omni pectore laetitias!
non iam illud quaero, contra me ut diligat illa,
aut, quod non potis est, esse pudica velit:
ipse valere opto et taetrum hunc deponere morbum.
o di, reddite mi hoc pro pietate mea.

LXXIX

Lesbius is handsome: why not? and Lesbia loves him
Better than you and all your family, Catullus.
But this handsome chap can sell Catullus and his family
If he can find three backers to vouch for him.

LXXX

How can I explain why your ordinarily red lips,
Gellius, become whiter than winter snow
When you leave home in the morning or wake from your siesta
In the long hours of the idle day?
There is something wrong somewhere: is it true what they say about you
That you like to devour an extended male member?
It must be that: as is declared by the unfortunate Victor's ruptured groin
And your lips smeared with the sperm you have milked from him.

LXXXI

Is there nowhere in all this crowd of people, Juventius,
Some handsome man you could decide to love
Other than this man you have let in from moribund Pisaurus?
He is paler than a gilded statue
And yet you love him and dare to prefer him to me:
Do you not realize what an appalling crime that is?

LXXXII

Quinti, si tibi vis oculos debere Catullum
   aut aliud siquid carius est oculis,
eripere ei noli, multo quod carius illi
   est oculis seu quid carius est oculis.

LXXXIII

Lesbia mi praesente viro mala plurima dicit:
   haec illi fatuo maxima laetitiast.
mule, nihil sentis. si nostri oblita taceret,
   sana esset: nunc quod gannit et obloquitur,
non solum meminit, sed quae multo acrior est res,
   iratast. hoc est, uritur et loquitur.

LXXXIV

Chommoda dicebat, si quando *commoda* vellet
   dicere, et *insidias* Arrius *hinsidias.*
et tum mirifice sperabat se esse locutum,
   cum quantum poterat dixerat *hinsidias.*
credo, sic mater, sic Liber avunculus eius,
   sic maternus avus dixerat atque avia.
hoc misso in Syriam requierant omnibus aures:
   audibant eadem haec leniter et leviter,
nec sibi postilla metuebant talia verba,
   cum subito affertur nuntius horribilis,
Ionios fluctus, postquam illuc Arrius isset,
   iam non *Iionios* esse, sed *Hionios.*

LXXXII

Quintius, if you want Catullus to owe his eyes to you,
Or something dearer than his eyes
Do not take from him what is dearer than his eyes
If there is something dearer to him than his eyes.

LXXXIII

In the presence of her husband Lesbia talks to me abusively:
And the fool thinks it is something to laugh about.
Mule, you have no sense. If she were to ignore me
She would be all right: the fact that she whines and scolds
Means that she not only remembers but—what is worse than that—
She is angry. That is, she burns as she talks.

LXXXIV

He used to say *honors* when he meant honors
Hambush when he meant ambush.
That was Arrius. He thought it was marvelous
If he said *hambush* at the top of his voice.
I imagine his mother and his uncle Liber,
His grandmother and his maternal grandfather spoke that way.
It gave everyone's ears a rest when he went to Syria;
Words were pronounced softly and lightly
And it seemed we were free of that sort of thing for the future.
Then suddenly the horrible news arrived:
The Ionian sea, as soon as Arrius got there,
Stopped being Ionian and became *Hionian.*

LXXXV

Odi et amo. quare id faciam, fortasse requiris.
nescio, sed fieri sentio et excrucior.

LXXXVI

Quintia formosast multis; mihi candida, longa,
rectast. haec ego sic singula confiteor,
totum illud formosa nego: nam nulla venustas,
nulla in tam magnost corpore mica salis.
Lesbia formosast, quae cum pulcherrima totast,
tum omnibus una omnis surripuit Veneres.

LXXXVII

Nulla potest mulier tantum se dicere amatam
vere, quantum a me Lesbia amata mea's.
nulla fides ullo fuit umquam foedere tanta,
quanta in amore tuo ex parte reperta meast.

LXXXVIII

Quid facit is, Gelli, qui cum matre atque sorore
prurit et abiectis pervigilat tunicis?
quid facit is, patruum qui non sinit esse maritum?
ecquid scis quantum suscipiat sceleris?
suscipit, o Gelli, quantum non ultima Tethys
nec genitor Nympharum abluit Oceanus:
nam nihil est quicquam sceleris quo prodeat ultra,
non si demisso se ipse voret capite.

LXXXV

I hate and I love. You may well ask, why I do so.
I do not know, but I feel it and suffer.

LXXXVI

Quintia is said to be beautiful. I would say tall, good complexion,
Well-built. I admit these attributes singly
But deny that they add up to beauty. She is not attractive:
In the whole of her large body there is not a grain of salt.
Lesbia is beautiful, totally and extremely so;
She has stolen all the attractions of all other women.

LXXXVII

No woman can say she was so much loved as you were,
Lesbia my darling, no one has loved as I have;
No trust was ever kept with such faith before
As, on my side, my love for you was kept.

LXXXVIII

What's Gellius up to? When he's with his mother and sister
He itches, and spends the evening with his clothes off.
What is he up to, not letting his uncle be married?
Do you know the extent of his turpitude?
There is so much of it, Gellius, that not even the ultimate Tethys
Can wash it away, or Oceanus who produced the nymphs:
There is no turpitude beyond it.
Not even if he were to put down his head and suck himself.

LXXXIX

Gellius est tenuis: quid ni? quoi tam bona mater
  tamque valens vivat tamque venusta soror
tamque bonus patruus tamque omnia plena puellis
  cognatis, quare is desinat esse macer?
qui ut nihil attingat, nisi quod fas tangere non est,
  quantumvis quare sit macer invenies.

XC

Nascatur magus ex Gelli matrisque nefando
  coniugio et discat Persicum aruspicium:
nam magus ex matre et gnato gignatur oportet,
  si verast Persarum impia religio,
gnatus ut accepto veneretur carmine divos
  omentum in flamma pingue liquefaciens.

XCI

Non ideo, Gelli, sperabam te mihi fidum
  in misero hoc nostro, hoc perdito amore fore,
quod te cognossem bene constantemve putarem
  aut posse a turpi mentem inhibere probro,
sed neque quod matrem nec germanam esse videbam
  hanc tibi, cuius me magnus edebat amor.
et quamvis tecum multo coniungerer usu,
  non satis id causae credideram esse tibi.
tu satis id duxti: tantum tibi gaudium in omni
  culpast, in quacumque est aliquid sceleris.

LXXXIX

Gellius is thin: why not? with such a kind mother
So fit and well, and such an attractive sister,
Such a very kind uncle and all those girls in the family,
How could he be otherwise than emaciated?
If he touched nothing but what is not legitimate to touch
There would still be plenty of reasons why he should be lean.

XC

A magus shoud be born of this unspeakable union
Of Gellius and his mother, and he should learn Persian fortunetelling:
For a magus has to be born of a mother and her son
If the blasphemous religion of the Persians is true
Or the child's hymns are not acceptable to the gods
As the guts melt greasily in the flame.

XCI

It was not, Gellius, that I hoped you would behave like a gentleman
In the matter of my miserable and uncontrolled love,
Nor because I knew you and imagined you were a solid character
Who could restrain your mind from any baseness,
But because it was neither your mother nor your sister
I was eating out my heart for:
And although we had been close friends
I did not think that would be reason enough for you.
But I was wrong: so much you delight in any weakness
In which there is a trace of vice.

XCII

Lesbia mi dicit semper male nec tacet umquam
  de me: Lesbia me dispeream nisi amat.
quo signo? quia sunt totidem mea: deprecor illam
  assidue, verum dispeream nisi amo.

XCIII

Nil nimium studeo, Caesar, tibi velle placere,
  nec scire utrum sis albus an ater homo.

XCIV

Mentula moechatur. moechatur mentula? certe
  hoc est quod dicunt, ipsa olera olla leigt.

XCV

Zmyrna mei Cinnae, nonam post denique messem
  quam coeptast nonamque edita post hiemem,
milia cum interea quingenta Hortensius uno

* * *

Zmyrna cavas Satrachi penitus mittetur ad undas,
  Zmyrnam cana diu saecula pervoluent.
at Volusi annales Paduam morientur ad ipsam
  et laxas scombris saepe dabunt tunicas.
parva mei mihi cordi monumenta sodalis,
  at populus tumido gaudeat Antimacho.

XCII

Lesbia is always talking scandal about me
And never stops: which proves that Lesbia loves me.
How does it prove it? I am in the same case: I abuse her
All the time: and one could not say I do not love her.

XCIII

It is indifferent to me whether I please you,
Caesar, or what is the color of your hair.

XCIV

John Thomas fucks. What could he do but fuck?
Do they not say, the pot finds its own stew?

XCV

Cinna's Smyrna, finished at last after nine summers
And given to the world after nine winters.
While meanwhile Hortensius has produced half a million lines

* * *

Smyrna will be diffused to the deep waters of Satrachus;
Gray-headed centuries will read Smyrna.
But the Annals of Volusius will end at Padua
Providing loose wrappings for mackerel.
My friend's small production will remain in my mind;
Let the public amuse themselves with the swollen Antimachus.

XCVI

Si quicquam mutis gratum acceptumve sepulcris
   accidere a nostro, Calve, dolore potest,
quo desiderio veteres renovamus amores
   atque olim amissas flemus amicitias,
certe non tanto mors immatura dolorist
   Quintiliae, quantum gaudet amore tuo.

XCVII

Non (ita me di ament) quicquam referre putavi,
   utrumne os an culum olfacerem Aemilio.
nilo mundius hoc, niloque immundius, illud,
   verum etiam culus mundior et melior:
nam sine dentibus est: os dentis sesquipedalis,
   gingivas vero ploxeni habet veteris,
praeterea rictum qualem diffissus in aestu
   meientis mulae cunnus habere solet.
hic futuit multas et se facit esse venustum,
   et non pistrino traditur atque asino?
quem siqua attingit, non illam posse putemus
   aegroti culum lingere carnificis?

XCVI

Calvus, if there is any pleasure for the dead
In our grief, or in the desire we have
To renew old loves,
Or in our mourning for our lost friendships
At least Quintilia must feel less grief at her early death
Than joy that you love her so much.

XCVII

So help me gods, I didn't think it mattered
Whether I smelt Aemilius's mouth or his arse:
One is no cleaner or dirtier than the other.
As a matter of fact the arse-hole is cleaner and pleasanter
Because it has no teeth. The mouth has teeth eighteen inches long,
Gums like an old wagonbox,
And gapes like the cunt of a pissing mule in summer.
This man fucks a lot of women and thinks himself charming:
He would be better employed driving a donkey round a millstone.
Any woman who touches him would be capable
Of licking the arse of a sick executioner.

XCVIII

In te, si in quemquam, dici pote, putide Victi,
  id quod verbosis dicitur et fatuis.
ista cum lingua, si usus veniat tibi, possis
  culos et crepidas lingere carpatinas.
si nos omnino vis omnes perdere, Victi,
  hiscas: omnino quod cupis efficies.

XCIX

Surripui tibi dum ludis, mellite Iuventi,
  saviolum dulci dulcius ambrosia.
verum id non impune tuli: namque amplius horam
  suffixum in summa me memini esse cruce,
dum tibi me purgo nec possum fletibus ullis
  tantillum vestrae demere saevitiae.
nam simul id factumst, multis diluta labella
  guttis abstersisti omnibus articulis,
ne quicquam nostro contractum ex ore maneret,
  tanquam commictae spurca saliva lupae.

* * *

praeterea infesto miserum me tradere Amori
  non cessasti omnique excruciare modo,
ut mi ex ambrosia mutatum iam foret illud
  saviolum tristi tristius helleboro.
quam quoniam poenam misero proponis amori
  numquam iam posthac basia surripiam.

XCVIII

It can be said of you if of any man, stinking Victius,
What they say about windbags and half-wits:
With a tongue like that, you could, if you get the chance,
Lick arses and farmers' boots.
If you want to kill the lot of us, Victius,
Whisper: you will achieve your objective perfectly.

XCIX

I kissed you while you were playing, sweet Juventius;
It was sweeter than the sweetest ambrosia.
I did not do it with impunity: for more than an hour,
I remember, it was as if I was hung up on a cross
And I could not talk myself out of it with tears
Or get the slightest reduction of your anger.
As soon as it was done you rinsed your lips with a lot of water
And wiped them with every joint of your fingers
So that nothing contracted from my mouth would remain
As if it were the filthy spit of a dirty whore.

* * *

Besides you forthwith handed me over to hostile love
And tortured me in every way
So that from being ambrosia that kiss was changed
Into the sharpest of sharp hellebore.
Since that is the penalty you exact for my unfortunate love
I will never steal kisses from you again.

C

Caelius Aufilenum et Quintius Aufilenam
  flos Veronensum depereunt iuvenum,
hic fratrem, ille sororem. hoc est, quod dicitur, illud
  fraternum vere dulce sodalitium.
cui faveam potius? Caeli, tibi: nam tua nobis
  perspecta egregiest unica amicitia,
cum vesana meas torreret flamma medullas.
  sis felix, Caeli, sis in amore potens.

CI

Multas per gentes et multa per aequora vectus
  advenio has miseras, frater, ad inferias,
ut te postremo donarem munere mortis
  et mutam nequiquam alloquerer cinerem,
quandoquidem fortuna mihi tete abstulit ipsum,
  heu miser indigne frater adempte mihi.
nunc tamen interea haec, prisco quae more parentum
  tradita sunt tristi munere ad inferias,
accipe fraterno multum manantia fletu,
  atque in perpetuum, frater, ave atque vale.

CII

Si quicquam tacite commissumst fido ab amico,
  cuius sit penitus nota fides animi,
meque esse invenies illorum iure sacratum,
  Corneli, et factum me esse puta Harpocratem.

C

Caelius is desperately in love with Aufilenus,
Quintius with Aufilena—the flower of Veronese youth,
The brother and the sister. This is indeed
The proverbial sweet companionship of brothers.
Which of them shall I favor? Caelius, you, because
You showed yourself preeminently friendly
When the insane fire was burning my marrow.
Be happy, Caelius, and potent in your love.

CI

Having come through many countries, over many seas,
I am here at last for these sad rites, my brother,
So that I may give you the gifts of death
And uselessly address your silent ashes:
Since fortune has carried you off
Alas, my brother, wrongfully taken from me,
Now take these offerings which, by ancestral custom,
Are given as a sad gift to the shades;
They are wet with your brother's tears:
And then forever, brother, hail and farewell.

CII

If any secret was ever told to a friend
And kept with profound loyalty,
You will find that I am of that persuasion,
Cornelius; you can think of me as a complete Harpocrates.

CIII

Aut, sodes, mihi redde decem sestertia, Silo,
deinde esto quamvis saevus et indomitus:
aut, si te nummi delectant, desine quaeso
leno esse atque idem saevus et indomitus.

CIV

Credis me potuisse meae malediciere vitae,
ambobus mihi quae carior est oculis?
non potui, nec si possem tam perdite amarem:
sed tu cum Tappone omnia monstra facis.

CV

Mentula conatur Pipleum scandere montem:
Musae furcillis praecipitem eiciunt.

CVI

Cum puero bello praeconem qui videt esse,
quid credat, nisi se vendere discupere?

CIII

Please either give me back my ten sestertia, Silo,
And then be as fierce and proud as you like
Or, if you're fond of money, give up, I beg of you,
Being a pimp and at the same time fierce and proud.

CIV

Do you believe I could have spoken ill of my life
Who is dearer to me than my two eyes?
I couldn't; and wouldn't love her so desperately if I could:
But you and Tappo make everything sound preposterous.

CV

Old cock tries to climb the Piplean hill;
The Muses however chuck him out with forks.

CVI

If you see a pretty boy with an auctioneer
Isn't it reasonable to think that he's for sale?

CVII

Sicui quid cupido optantique optigit umquam
   insperanti, hoc est gratum animo proprie.
quare hoc est gratum nobis quoque, carius auro,
   quod te restituis, Lesbia, mi cupido,
restituis cupido atque insperanti, ipsa refers te
   nobis: o lucem candidiore nota!
quis me uno vivit felicior, aut magis hac rem
   optandam in vita dicere quis poterit?

CVIII

Si, Comini, populi arbitrio tua cana senectus
   spurcata impuris moribus intereat,
non equidem dubito quin primum inimica bonorum
   lingua execta avido sit data vulturio,
effossos oculos voret atro gutture corvus,
   intestina canes, cetera membra lupi.

CIX

Iucundum, mea vita, mihi proponis amorem
   hunc nostrum inter nos perpetuumque fore.
di magni, facite ut vere promittere possit,
   atque id sincere dicat et ex animo,
ut liceat nobis tota perducere vita
   aeternum hoc sanctae foedus amicitiae.

CVII

When something happens you wanted and never hoped for
That is, in the exact sense, a pleasure to the mind.
And so to me it is a pleasure more precious than gold
That you, Lesbia, return to me who desire you,
Desire but have given up hoping; give yourself back
To me: it is a day for a whiter mark.
What man alive is happier than I, or could say
There is anything more to be desired in this life?

CVIII

If, Cominius, by the will of the people your gray age
And filthy practices were brought to an end,
I have no doubt that first, your slanderous tongue
Would be cut out and given to a hungry vulture,
Your eyes gouged out and devoured by a black-throated crow,
Your entrails given to the dogs, the rest to the wolves.

CIX

My life, you promise that this love of ours
Shall be agreeable and last forever:
Great gods, arrange for her to speak the truth
And make this promise without reservation
So that we may protract though all our life
This treaty of inviolable friendship.

CX

Aufilena, bonae semper laudantur amicae:
  accipiunt pretium quae facere instituunt.
tu, quod promisti mihi quod mentire, inimica's:
  quod nec das et fers, turpe facis facinus.
aut facere ingenuae est aut non promisse pudicae,
  Aufilena, fuit: sed data corripere
fraudando officium est plus quam meretricis avarae,
  quae sese toto corpore prostituit.

CXI

Aufilena, viro contentam vivere solo,
  nuptarumst laus e laudibus eximiis:
sed quoivis quamvis potius succumbere par est,
  quam matrem fratres ex patruo parere.

CXII

Multus homo es, Naso, neque tecum multus homost qui
  descendit: Naso, multus es et pathicus.

CXIII

Consule Pompeio primum duo, Cinna, solebant
  Maeciliam: facto consule nunc iterum
manserunt duo, sed creverunt milia in unum
  singula. fecundum semen adulterio.

CX

Aufilena, kind girls are always well spoken of;
They get the money and they do what they say they will.
You are more of a girl-enemy than a girl-friend:
You promise, lie, give nothing and take all.
You are entitled either to do it or to be chaste and not promise,
But, Aufilena, to snatch all you can get
And then cheat, is to be worse than a greedy whore
Who prostitutes herself with her whole body.

CXI

Aufilena, it is creditable in the highest degree
For a bride to be content with one husband:
But it is better to lie down with all comers
Than to produce brothers who are also cousins.

CXII

You are stuck-up, Naso, and the man who is not stuck up
Goes down with you: you are stuck up and a pathic.

CXIII

In Pompey's first consulship, Cinna, two men
Frequented Maecilia: now that he is consul again
The two are still there, but beside each of them has sprung up
A thousand. Adultery is very fruitful.

CXIV

Firmano saltu non falso Mentula dives
 fertur, qui tot res in se habet egregias,
aucupia omne genus, piscis, prata, arva ferasque.
 nequiquam: fructus sumptibus exuperat.
quare concedo sit dives, dum omnia desint.
 saltus laudemus commoda, dum ipse egeat.

CXV

Mentula habet instar triginta iugera prati,
 quadraginta arvi: cetera sunt maria.
cur non divitiis Croesum superare potis sit
 uno qui in saltu totmoda possideat,
prata, arva, ingentis silvas saltusque paludesque
 usque ad Hyperboreos et mare ad Oceanum?
omnia magna haec sunt; tamen ipsest maximus, alter
 non homo sed vero mentula magna minax.

CXVI

Saepe tibi studioso animo venante requirens
 carmina uti possem mittere Battiadae,
qui te lenirem nobis, neu conarere
 tela infesta mihi mittere in usque caput,
hunc video mihi nunc frustra sumptum esse laborem,
 Gelli, nec nostras hic valuisse preces.
contra nos tela ista tua evitamus amictu:
 at fixus nostris tu dabi' supplicium.

CXIV

Cock is said to be rich with his estate at Firmum.
It is true, there are all kinds of marvelous things on it,
Game of all kinds, fish, ploughland and pasture.
It is no good: the expenses outrun the produce.
So I admit he is rich, but somehow everything is lacking.
We can admire the wealth of the estate as long as he remains poor.

CXV

Cock has something like thirty acres of pasture,
Forty arable, and the rest is salt water.
How could he fail to surpass Croesus in wealth
Who possesses so many things on one estate,
Pasture, arable, immense woods and then marshes
Stretching to the Hyperboreans and the Great Sea?
They are very big, but he is the biggest of all,
Not a man at all but a huge menacing cock.

CXVI

I have often considered in my studious way
How I could possibly send you some poems of Callimachus
Which would soothe you, so that you did not attempt
To threaten me all the time with your hostile weapons.
Now I see that I have done all this work for nothing,
Gellius, and that my prayers have got nowhere.
I will draw my cloak about me to avoid your weapons
But fixed by mine you shall be put to the torture.

FRAGMENTA

Porphyrion ad Hor. *C. I.* 16. 22:

1. At non effugies meo iambos.

Terentianus Maurus 2755–8 (p. 406 Keil):

2. Hunc lucum tibi dedico consecroque Priape,
   qua domus tua Lampsacist quaque silva, Priape,
   nam te praecipue in suis urbibus colit ora
   Hellespontia ceteris ostreosior oris.

Nonius, p. 200 Linds: Catullus Priapo:

3. – ⏑ – ⏑⏑ de meo ligurrire libidost.

FRAGMENTS

1. But you shall not escape my iambics

2. This place I dedicate and consecrate
To you, Priapus, at Lampsacus which is your home
Because on the shores of the Hellespont you are especially worshiped
On account of the plentiful supply of oysters.

3. at my own cost it is a pleasure to lick up

Note on XVI

Some additional lines, not in Loeb, are given in a number of editions. I have not included them in my text because it seems to me that the poem is better without them. In the shorter version Catullus is making a point (as always); the additional lines are probably spurious. It is unlike Catullus to exalt the pornographic quality of what he wrote; his mind was too much on his subject. I give here a translation of the lines in question.

Since they have salt and charm
And are lascivious and lacking in reserve
And can excite a certain itching,
I do not say in boys, but in hairy men
Who can scarcely move their stiff loins,
You, because you read about thousands of kisses
Think I myself must be effeminate.
All right, I'll bugger you and suck your pricks.

VALEDICTION

Catullus my friend across twenty centuries,
Anxious to complete your lechery before Christ came.

This book was composed on the linotype
in Caledonia. A modified Scotch face,
which accounts for the name, it first
appeared in 1949.

Composed, printed and bound by H. Wolff
Book Manufacturing Company, Inc., New York.

Designed by Jacqueline Schuman.